japan & korea

To Reuben, who married me before I learned to cook.

Completely revised and updated in 2011
First published in 1976

This edition published in 2013 by Hardie Grant Books

Hardie Grant Books (Australia)
Ground Floor, Building 1
658 Church Street
Richmond, Victoria 3121
www.hardiegrant.com.au

Hardie Grant Books (UK)
Dudley House, North Suite
34–35 Southampton Street
London WC2E 7HF
www.hardiegrant.co.uk

A Cataloguing-in-Publication entry is available from the catalogue of the National Library of
Australia at www.nla.gov.au
The Complete Asian Cookbook: Japan & Korea
ISBN 978 1 74270 683 2

Publishing Director: Paul McNally
Project Editor: Rihana Ries
Editor: Ariana Klepac
Design Manager: Heather Menzies
Design Concept: Murray Batten
Typesetting: Megan Ellis
Photographer: Alan Benson
Stylist: Vanessa Austin
Production: Todd Rechner

Colour reproduction by Splitting Image Colour Studio
Printed and bound in China by 1010 Printing International Limited

Find this book on **Cooked.**

THE
Complete
Asian
COOKBOOK

japan &
korea

CHARMAINE SOLOMON

hardie grant books
MELBOURNE · LONDON

Contents

Foreword

Just as France has its robust country fare as well as its subtle haute cuisine, so too does Asia have a range of culinary delights that can be simple, complex, fiery, mild, tantalising — and compulsive! Not all Asian food is exotic or wildly unusual. Noodle and rice dishes are as commonplace as the pastas and potatoes of the West. Many of the ingredients will be familiar to anyone who knows their way around a kitchen. The main differences have arisen just as they have arisen in other parts of the world — through the use of available ingredients. Thus there is a reliance on some herbs and spices less well known in the West. Meat is often replaced by the nutritious by-products of the soy bean and by protein-rich fish sauces and shrimp pastes.

True, some of the more unusual ingredients take a little getting used to. But once you have overcome what resistance you may have towards the idea of raw fish or dried shrimp paste or seaweed, you'll find that these (and other) ingredients are no less delicious than – and certainly as exciting as – those you use in your favourite dishes.

The introduction to these countries will give you a good idea of what to expect in the way of out-of-the-ordinary ingredients. Almost without exception, those called for are readily available in most large supermarkets or Asian grocery stores; in the rare case they are not, suitable substitutes have been given.

Those of you already familiar with Japanese and Korean cuisine will, I hope, find recipes to interest and excite you in these pages; and I think you will be tempted to explore dishes with which you are less well acquainted. For those of you who are coming to Japanese and Korean cooking for the first time, I have taken care to make sure the essential steps are clear and precise, with detailed instructions on the following pages for cooking the much-used ingredients (such as rice, noodles and chilli), and pointers on how to joint a chicken, portion fish and select and season a wok.

For most recipes, the names have been given in the dominant or most common language or dialect of the country concerned, followed by the English name in italics. Generally, the letter 'a' in Japanese and Korean words is pronounced as the 'a' in father, never as in cat; and the letter 'u' is rather like the 'oo' in look, never as in duty.

Eating for health

Most Asian food is healthy. Many spices and ingredients such as garlic and ginger have proven health-giving properties. However, with today's emphasis on weight control I have made modifications in the quantity and type of fat used for cooking. I have found it is possible to get very good results using almost half the amount of fat called for in many traditional dishes.

All of these recipes are adaptable to low-fat diets with very little sacrifice of flavour, since most of the exotic tastes come from herbs, spices and sauces.

Cooking with a wok

If I had to choose one cooking pan to be marooned on a desert island with, I'd choose a wok. It would cope with any kind of food that happened to be available. In it you can boil, braise, fry and steam, and while you can do all these things in pans you already possess, the wok is almost indispensable for the stir-frying technique that many Asian dishes call for. Because of its rounded shape and high, flaring sides you can toss with abandon and stir-fry ingredients without their leaping over the sides; and because the wok is made of thin iron you get the quick, high heat necessary to much Asian cooking.

Though a wok is best used with gas, it is possible to get good results with electricity. Because quick, high heat is required in stir-frying, turn the hotplate on to the highest heat and place the wok directly on it; it is possible to buy woks with a flat base for better contact, or invest in an electric wok where the heating element is built into the pan. The 30–35 cm (12–14 in) wok is most useful. You can cook small quantities in a large wok, but not vice versa.

The wok made of stainless steel is a modern innovation, but a modestly priced iron wok heats up quickly and evenly and, if you remember to dry it well after washing, it will not rust.

Before use, an iron wok must be seasoned. Prepare it by washing thoroughly in hot water and detergent. Some woks, when new, have a lacquer-like coating, which must be removed by almost filling the wok with water, adding about 2 tablespoons bicarbonate of soda (baking soda) and boiling for about 15 minutes. This softens the coating and it can be scrubbed off with a fine scourer. If some of the coating still remains, repeat the process until the wok is free from any lacquer on the inside. To season the new wok, dry it well, put over gentle heat and, when the metal heats up, wipe over the entire inner surface with some crumpled paper towel dipped in peanut oil. Repeat a number of times with more oil-soaked paper until the paper stays clean. Allow to cool. Your wok is now ready for use.

After cooking in it, do not scrub the wok with steel wool or abrasives of any kind. Soak in hot water to soften any remaining food, then rub gently with a sponge, using hot water and detergent – this preserves the surface. Make sure the wok is quite dry, because if moisture stays left in the pan it will rust. Heat the wok gently to ensure complete dryness, then rub over the inside surface with lightly oiled paper. A well-used wok will soon turn black, but this is normal – and the more a wok is used, the better it is to cook in.

Deep-frying

A wok is an efficient pan for deep-frying as it has a wider surface area than a regular frying pan. Be sure that the wok is sitting securely on the stove. Fill the wok no more than two-thirds full and heat the oil over medium heat.

To check the temperature for deep-frying, use a kitchen thermometer if you have one – on average, 180°C (350°F) is the correct temperature. To test without a thermometer, a cube of bread dropped into the oil will brown in 15 seconds at 180°C (350°F), and in 10 seconds if the temperature is 190°C (375°F).

The higher temperature may be suitable to use for foods that don't have great thickness, such as pappadams or seafood tempura, but if something needs to cook through, such as chicken pieces, use a lower temperature of around 160°C (320°F) – in this case a cube of bread will take nearly 30 seconds to brown. If the temperature is not hot enough, the food will absorb oil and become greasy. If you overheat the oil it could catch fire.

Use refined peanut oil, light olive oil, canola or rice bran oil and lower the food in gently with tongs or a slotted spoon so as not to splash yourself with hot oil. Removing the fried food to a colander lined with crumpled paper towel will help to remove any excess oil.

After cooling, oil may be poured through a fine metal skimmer and stored in an airtight jar away from the light. It may be used within a month or so, adding fresh oil to it when heating. After a couple of uses, it will need to be disposed of properly.

Chillies

Fresh chillies are used in most Asian food. If mild flavouring is required, simply wash the chilli and add it to the dish when simmering, then lift out and discard the chilli before serving. But if you want the authentic fiery quality of the dish, you need to seed and chop the chillies first. To do this, remove the stalk of each chilli and cut in half lengthways to remove the central membrane and seeds – the seeds are the hottest part of the chilli.

If you handle chillies without wearing gloves, wash your hands thoroughly with soap and warm water afterwards. Chillies can be so hot that even two or three good washings do not stop the tingling sensation, which can go on for hours. If this happens, remember to keep your hands well away from your eyes, lips or where the skin is especially sensitive. If you have more chillies than you need, they can be wrapped in plastic wrap and frozen, then added to dishes and used without thawing.

Dried chillies come in many shapes and sizes. Generally I use the large variety. If frying them as an accompaniment to a meal, use them whole, dropping them straight into hot oil. If they are being soaked and ground, first cut off the stalk end and shake the chilli so that the seeds fall out. They are safe enough to handle until they have been soaked and ground, but if you handle them after this has been done, remember to wash your hands at once with soap and water.

Dried chillies, though they give plenty of heat and flavour, do not have the same volatile oils as fresh chillies and so do not have as much effect on the skin.

Rice varieties

One of the oldest grains in the world, and a staple food of more than half the world's population, rice is by far the most important item in the daily diet throughout Asia.

There are thousands of varieties. Agricultural scientists involved in producing new and higher yielding strains of rice will pick differences that are not apparent to even the most enthusiastic rice eater. But, from the Asian consumer's viewpoint, rice has qualities that a Westerner might not even notice – colour, fragrance, flavour, texture.

Rice buyers are so trained to recognise different types of rice that they can hold a few grains in the palm to warm it, sniff it through the hole made by thumb and forefinger, and know its age, variety, even perhaps where it was grown. Old rice is sought after and prized more than new rice because it tends to be fluffy and separate when cooked, even if the cook absent-mindedly adds too much water. Generally speaking, the white polished grains – whether long and fine or small and pearly (much smaller than what we know as short-grain rice) – are considered best.

Further east, medium- or short-grain varieties come into their own. In Korea and Japan they prefer rice that is perfectly cooked but not dry and fluffy. Glossy, pearly grains are desired, each one well defined, but with a tendency to cling together so that it can easily be picked up with chopsticks. No salt is used.

Rice is sold either packaged or in bulk. Polished white rice is available as long-, medium- or short-grain. Unpolished or natural rice is available as medium- or long-grain; and in many countries it is possible to buy an aromatic table rice grown in Bangladesh, called basmati rice. In dishes where spices and flavourings are added and cooked with the rice, any type of long-grain rice may be used. In each recipe the type of rice best suited is recommended, but as a general rule, remember that medium-grain or short-grain rice gives a clinging result and long-grain rice, properly cooked, is fluffy and separate.

Preparing rice

To wash or not to wash? Among Asian cooks there will never be agreement on whether rice should be washed or not. Some favour washing the rice several times, then leaving it to soak for a while. Other good cooks insist that washing rice is stupid and wasteful, taking away what vitamins and nutrients are left after the milling process.

I have found that most rice sold in Australia does not need washing but that rice imported in bulk and packaged here picks up a lot of dust and dirt and needs thorough washing and draining.

In a recipe, if rice is to be fried before any liquid is added, the washed rice must be allowed enough time to thoroughly drain and dry, between 30 and 60 minutes. Rice to be steamed must be soaked overnight. Rice for cooking by the absorption method may be washed (or not), drained briefly and added to the pan immediately.

Cooking rice

For a fail-safe way of cooking rice perfectly every time, put the required amount of rice and water into a large saucepan with a tight-fitting lid (see the measures above right). Bring to the boil over high heat, cover, then reduce the heat to low and simmer for 20 minutes. Remove from the heat, uncover the pan and allow the steam to escape for a few minutes before fluffing up the rice with a fork.

Transfer the rice to a serving dish with a slotted metal spoon – don't use a wooden spoon or it will crush the grains. You will notice that long-grain rice absorbs considerably more water than short-grain rice, so the two kinds are not interchangeable in recipes. Though details are given in every rice recipe, here is a general rule regarding proportions of rice and liquid.

Long-grain rice	Short- or medium-grain rice
200 g (7 oz/1 cup) rice use 500 ml (17 fl oz/2 cups) water	220 g (8 oz/1 cup) rice use 375 ml (12½ fl oz/1½ cups) water
400 g (14 oz/2 cups) rice use 875 ml (29½ fl oz/3½ cups) water	440 g (15½ oz/2 cups) rice use 625 ml (21 fl oz/2½ cups) water
600 g (1 lb 5 oz/3 cups) rice use 1.25 litres (42 fl oz/5 cups) water	660 g (1 lb 7 oz/3 cups) rice use 875 ml (29½ fl oz/3½ cups) water
Use 500 ml (17 fl oz/2 cups) water for the first cup of rice, then 375 ml (12½ fl oz/1½ cups) water for each additional cup of rice.	Use 375 ml (12½ fl oz/1½ cups) water for the first cup of rice, then 250 ml (8½ fl oz/1 cup) water for each additional cup of rice.

Noodles

There are many different types of noodles available and different Asian countries have specific uses and preferences. Almost all of these varieties are available from large supermarkets or Asian grocery stores.

Dried egg noodles: Perhaps the most popular noodles, these are made of wheat flour. Dried egg noodles must be soaked in hot water for about 10 minutes before cooking. This is not mentioned in the cooking instructions, yet it does make cooking them so much easier – as the noodles soften the strands spread and separate and the noodles cook more evenly than when they are dropped straight into boiling water.

A spoonful of oil in the water prevents boiling over. When water returns to the boil, cook fine noodles for 2–3 minutes and thick noodles for 3–4 minutes. Do not overcook. Drain immediately, then run cold water through the noodles to rinse off any excess starch and cool them so they don't continue to cook in their own heat. Drain thoroughly. To reheat, pour boiling water over the noodles in a colander. Serve with stir-fried dishes or use in soups and braised noodle dishes.

Dried rice noodles: There are various kinds of flat rice noodles. Depending on the type of noodle and thickness of the strands, they have to be soaked in cold water for 30–60 minutes before cooking. Drain, then drop into a saucepan of boiling water and cook for 6–10 minutes, testing every minute after the first 6 minutes so you will know when they are done. As soon as they are tender, drain in a colander and rinse well in cold running water. Drain once more. They can then be fried or heated in soup before serving.

Dried rice vermicelli (rice-stick) noodles: Rice vermicelli has very fine strands and cooks very quickly. Drop into boiling water and cook for 2–3 minutes only. Drain well. Serve in soups or with dishes that have a good amount of sauce. Or, if a crisp garnish is required, use rice vermicelli straight from the packet and deep-fry small amounts for just a few seconds. It will puff and become white as soon as it is immersed in the oil if it is hot enough. Lift out quickly on a slotted spoon or wire strainer and drain on paper towels before serving.

Dried cellophane (bean thread) noodles: Also known as bean starch noodles, these dried noodles need to be soaked in hot water for 20 minutes, then drained and cooked in a saucepan of boiling water for 15 minutes, or until tender. For use as a crisp garnish, deep-fry them in hot oil straight from the packet, as for rice vermicelli (above). In Japan they have a similar fine translucent noodle, known as harusame.

Preparing soft-fried noodles

After the noodles have been boiled and drained, spread them on a large baking tray lined with paper towel and leave them to dry for at least 30 minutes – a little peanut oil may be sprinkled over them to prevent sticking. Heat 2 tablespoons each of peanut oil and sesame oil in a wok or large heavy-based frying pan until hot, then add a handful of noodles and cook until golden on one side. Turn and cook the other side until golden, then remove to a plate. Repeat with the remaining noodles. It may be necessary to add more oil to the wok if a large quantity of noodles is being fried, but make sure the fresh oil is very hot first. Serve with beef, pork, poultry or vegetable dishes.

Preparing crisp-fried noodles

Rice vermicelli (rice-stick) and cellophane (bean thread) noodles can be fried in hot oil straight from the packet. Egg noodles need to be cooked first, then drained and spread out on a large baking tray lined with paper towel to dry for at least 30 minutes – a little peanut oil can be sprinkled over them to prevent sticking. Heat sufficient peanut oil in a wok or heavy-based frying pan over medium heat. When the oil is hot, deep-fry the noodles, in batches, until crisp and golden brown. Drain on paper towel. These crisp noodles are used mainly as a garnish.

Preparing whole chickens

Jointing a chicken

I have often referred to cutting a chicken into serving pieces suitable for a curry. This is simply cutting the pieces smaller than joints so that the spices can more readily penetrate and flavour the meat.

To joint a chicken, first cut off the thighs and drumsticks, then separate the drumsticks from the thighs. Cut off the wings and divide them at the middle joint (wing tips may be added to a stock but do not count as a joint). The breast is divided down the centre into two, then across into four pieces – do not start cooking the breast pieces at the same time as the others, but add them later, as breast meat has a tendency to become dry if cooked for too long.

A 1.5 kg (3 lb 5 oz) chicken, for instance, can be jointed, then broken down further into serving pieces. The thighs are cut into two with a heavy cleaver; the back is cut into four pieces and used in the curry, though not counted as serving pieces because there is very little meat on them. Neck and giblets are also included to give extra flavour.

Preparing whole fish

Cutting fish fillets into serving pieces

Fish fillets are of varying thickness, length and density. For example, whole fillets of flathead can be dipped in tempura batter and will cook in less than a minute in hot oil, whereas a fillet of ling or trevalla will need to be cut into 3 cm (1¼ in) strips for the same recipe.

Let common sense prevail when portioning fish fillets, but always remember that fish is cooked when the flesh turns opaque when flaked with a fork or knife.

Cutting fish steaks into serving pieces

Depending on the size of the fish, each steak may need to be cut into four, six or eight pieces. Once again, smaller portions are better, for they allow flavours to penetrate and you can allow more than one piece per person. The accompanying sketch shows how to divide fish steaks – small ones into four pieces, medium-sized ones into six pieces and really large steaks into eight pieces.

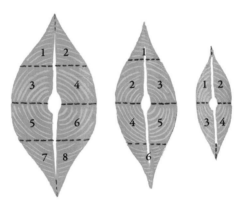

Japan

Japanese food stands apart from all other Asian food because of its simplicity and purity. It is memorable not for its spicing or richness or complex blending of flavours, but because it emphasises basic ingredients and trains the palate to accept and appreciate food in its most natural state.

To those brought up in a tradition of cooking that prides itself on subtle sauces or spice blends that tantalise and defy analysis, this sparseness of seasoning may come as something of a surprise. But once Japanese food has been approached without prejudice, and sampled with good appetite and an open mind, it wins admirers from all culinary backgrounds. To think I once imagined I wouldn't enjoy raw fish! Nothing in any other cuisine approaches the silkiness of pale pink salmon or buttery tuna belly (*toro*) sashimi. It has to be experienced to be believed. And it goes without saying that any seafood for sashimi needs to be premium quality and super fresh. There are no strong, fishy tastes because only the choicest portions of the freshest fish are used. It is a dish for the connoisseur with a discerning palate, the dipping sauces of soy and wasabi and perhaps a shiso leaf adding flavour without masking the taste of the fish itself.

What is the special quality of Japanese cooking? Is it the beautiful presentation? Is it the small quantities in which food is served so that one appreciates the appearance, aroma, taste and texture in a special way? I think it is all these – and a certain attitude that the Japanese have towards food. It is considered not only fuel for the body but also food for the soul. There is as much attention given to the right bowl or plate on which to present the food, and the arrangement of the food on that plate, as to the preparation of the food itself. The surroundings in which a meal is eaten are also carefully chosen so that a peaceful atmosphere prevails. An alcove in the room will provide a setting for a simple *ikebana* arrangement. A Japanese meal should be an experience for all the senses.

Great emphasis is placed on freshness, quality and foods in season. Japanese cooks shop every day so they are certain of the freshness of ingredients. The first of any seasonal food is always greatly prized, and they are prepared to pay high prices for the privilege of tasting the first strawberries, matsutake mushrooms or other seasonal treats.

Comparing Japanese cooking with other Asian cooking, another difference is that most traditional Japanese cooking is done in or over water, while other cuisines use oil as a cooking medium. Water-based cooking gives a lightness and delicacy of flavour that is most appealing. Steaming means that the pure flavours of the food and most of the nutrient value are retained.

Seaweed may not be everyone's cup of dashi, but when used as a flavouring for rice, stock and other dishes, it is so subtle as to be hardly discernible. Similarly, *katsuobushi*, dried, smoked and thinly shaved bonito, delivers an intriguing complexity to the stocks and sauces it is simmered in. Toasted nori, a great favourite in Japan, is prized for its strong flavour. Wakame, a seaweed popular in soups and other simmered dishes, has an unmistakably marine smell and taste. Seaweed salad may not sound appetising, but the finely shredded bright green sea vegetable, tossed in a delicious dressing that includes sesame oil, mirin, rice vinegar and shoyu (Japanese soy sauce), packs a flavour punch and a tender crunch unlike anything else I have tasted.

Tofu or soy bean curd, low in kilojoules (calories) and high in protein, is a mainstay of the Japanese diet. It is served at breakfast, lunch and dinner. Its flavour is so delicate that it might be mistaken for a custard that is neither sweet nor savoury, but once someone takes a liking to this food, it becomes almost a fetish.

Miso (fermented soy bean paste) and shoyu are two more soy bean products that are fundamental to Japanese cuisine. Japanese soy sauce is the most universally used seasoning and who, having savoured the wonderful difference it makes to all kinds of food, would be content to do without it?

Perhaps the best feature of Japanese food is that it is so light. Even deep-fried foods such as tonkatsu or tempura are renowned for their lightness. Tempura batter is feather-light and so thin that it is almost transparent, providing a crisp coating that helps the food cook both in the hot oil and in its own steam within the fragile batter covering. Pure vegetable oil is used for frying, and is usually a mixture of different oils such as corn oil, olive oil and a proportion of sesame oil for flavour. It is heated to just the right temperature to keep fried food digestible and non-greasy.

Although tempura is widely known, and is one of the most popular Japanese dishes, it is a comparatively recent addition to Japan's cuisine, having been introduced by the Portuguese in the sixteenth century. On days when, as Catholics, they were forbidden to eat meat, they asked for prawns (shrimp) fried in batter. What the Japanese did with the basic idea was to refine it, create a batter of exquisite lightness and make the cooking and serving of it a triumph of split-second timing.

'Aesthetic' is the word that best describes Japanese food, because along with freshness and flavour is an awareness of how food should be presented. This changes with the seasons. The Japanese don't try to impress with imported, out-of-season delicacies, but celebrate the seasons, making the most of the foods when nature provides them. A seasonal motif, such as a slice of carrot shaped like a blossom in springtime, or in autumn carved to resemble a maple leaf, reflects a changing of moods. Summer foods, cool and light, are set off by green leaves and delicate plates, while winter brings on steaming *nabemono* foods such as shabu-shabu and sukiyaki, to be cooked and eaten at the table.

Even the plates and dishes for serving and eating are chosen for their seasonal suitability. This awareness of the changing of the seasons permeates Japanese culture and thinking, and the choice and presentation of food. The Japanese word for this seasonal feeling is *kisetsukan*. It is virtually impossible for someone who has not lived in Japan and experienced this first-hand to understand and express this heightened awareness. But happily it is possible, without too much trouble, to cook Japanese food and enjoy it.

Great importance is attached to the cooking of rice, for if there is one thing the Japanese home cook must be able to do, it is to cook rice and cook it perfectly. Nowadays, automatic rice cookers are widely used, but for centuries rice was cooked without these modern marvels and has always been cooked well. The absorption method is used; though slightly different from the methods used in other Asian countries, the recipe on page 17 is simple and always gives good results.

Serving and eating a Japanese meal

Unlike Chinese meals where the effect is lavish, with large serving dishes holding quantities of food, Japanese meals are usually served on individual dishes in small servings. Sometimes a tray is set in front of each diner, with all the food served at one time, but each dish on its own carefully chosen plate or bowl.

Soup is served in covered bowls. Japanese lacquer bowls with covers keep the soup hot but must be handled carefully, for the steam forms a seal; to release the seal, squeeze the bowl gently or the soup will spill while you try to prise off the cover. Chopsticks are used to pick up any ingredients added to the soup, then the bowl is lifted to the lips with both hands. No spoons are used for any Japanese food except *chawan mushi* (steamed savoury custard). Japanese chopsticks are more pointed than Chinese ones, and are generally made from lacquered wood. In most restaurants, however, wooden chopsticks (*warabashi*) are used; they come sealed in a paper envelope, and are thrown away after use. Although rice is of prime importance, noodles of various kinds are sometimes served instead; chilled noodle dishes are especially popular in summer.

Sake or tea is served with meals. In summer a popular beverage is *mugicha*, or iced 'tea', made not with tea but with roasted unhusked barley brewed like tea. It is refreshing and, though the first sip may taste strange, it is a drink that most people grow to like. It is also very popular in Korea, and I have been served it both in Japanese and Korean homes.

When sake is served in winter, the bottle or flask is put in hot water until it warms up to 43°C (109°F). Tiny cups called *sakazuki* are used for drinking the sake, but liqueur glasses may be used instead. In summer the sake may be served chilled.

Utensils

While there are special utensils traditionally used in Japanese cooking, it is reassuring to know that in modern Japanese homes electric frying pans and automatic rice cookers are preferred. Heavy-based saucepans with tight-fitting lids and other good-quality cookware normally found in Western kitchens cope adequately with any of the Japanese dishes in this book.

The one pan that would not be found in a Western kitchen is the rectangular omelette pan used for making rolled omelettes. It is naturally easier to achieve an even roll in one of these than in a round pan and, if you're keen on buying one, some Japanese grocery stores sell them. A sharp chopper or really good kitchen knife and other utensils you are most at home with, are the best ones to use. You may want to invest in a ceramic Japanese grater if you don't own one that grates finely enough. For cooking at the table there are many useful and decorative pans available. If you are keen to make sushi, get yourself a few bamboo mats (*maki-sudare*).

Your Japanese Shelf

These ingredients will put an entire range of Japanese dishes at your fingertips. Fresh ingredients are not included, only those that have a good shelf life. Buy in small quantities and store in airtight jars away from heat and direct sunlight.

aburage (deep-fried tofu sheets)

atsuage/namaage (deep-fried pressed tofu)

bonito flakes (*katsuobushi*), dried and smoked

fish cakes, Japanese-style (*kamaboko*)

ginkgo nuts

gomashio (sesame salt)

kombu (dried kelp)

mirin (sweet rice wine)

miso (fermented soy bean paste)

noodles – harusame, soba (buckwheat noodles), somen, udon

panko (Japanese breadcrumbs)

takuan (pickled daikon/white radish)

pickled ginger (*beni shoga*)

rice vinegar

sake (dry rice wine)

sansho (Japanese pepper)

sesame oil

shiitake mushrooms, dried

shirataki noodles

shiso (a strongly flavoured, large-leafed herb traditionally eaten with raw fish)

shoyu (Japanese soy sauce)

wasabi paste

Rice
and
Noodles

❖

Gohan
Cooked rice

Serves: 6

White rice cooked by the absorption method is the staple food of Japan, and short- or medium-grain varieties are preferred. Rice is made up into other dishes with vegetables, fish or meat but most often it is served as the mainstay of the meal with which other dishes are eaten. An automatic rice cooker, which ensures perfectly cooked rice every time, is almost an essential kitchen appliance, but just as reliable is this traditional method.

550 g (1 lb 3 oz/2½ cups) short-grain rice

Wash the rice well and drain in a colander for 30 minutes. Put the rice into a heavy-based saucepan with a tight-fitting lid, add 750 ml (25½ fl oz/3 cups) cold water and bring to the boil. Reduce the heat to low, cover, and steam for 15 minutes without lifting the lid. Turn the heat to high for 20 seconds still with the pan covered, remove the pan from the heat and allow to stand for 10 minutes before serving. Dipping a rice paddle in cold water before each serving prevents cooked rice grains sticking to it.

Musubi
Rice balls

Makes: 4

Rice balls are usually taken on picnics and are sometimes filled with pieces of raw or smoked fish. They may also be very simply flavoured with sesame seeds or seaweed.

370 g (13 oz/2 cups) cooked short-grain rice (above)

gomashio or powdered nori to coat

raw or smoked fish, thinly sliced (optional)

When the rice is cool enough to handle, take about 95 g (3¼ oz/½ cup) at a time and, with wet hands, roll into firm balls with a 7.5 cm (3 in) diameter. If using fish, push a strip into the centre of each rice ball, moulding the rice around it. Roll the rice balls lightly in gomashio or powdered nori to coat.

Oyako Domburi
Parent and child domburi

Serves: 6

Domburi means an earthenware bowl, but the name also applies to the food served in it, generally rice with toppings of meat, eggs, poultry, vegetables or a combination of ingredients. *Oyako domburi* is so called because it is made from chicken and eggs served over rice.

500 ml (17 fl oz/2 cups) Chicken stock (page 32)

1 tablespoon mirin

125 ml (4 fl oz/½ cup) shoyu (Japanese soy sauce)

500 g (1 lb 2 oz) boneless skinless chicken breasts or thighs, diced

6 eggs, lightly beaten

¼ teaspoon salt

6 spring onions (scallions), thinly sliced

1 quantity cooked short-grain rice (page 17)

Put the chicken stock, mirin and shoyu in a saucepan and bring to the boil. Add the chicken, return to the boil, then reduce the heat to low, cover, and simmer for 8 minutes.

Meanwhile, season the egg with the salt, then add the egg and three-quarters of the spring onion to the simmering stock. Without stirring, let the mixture return to the boil, then reduce the heat to low, cover, and cook for 3–4 minutes, or until the eggs are set but still soft.

Spoon the rice into a heated earthenware bowl, then pour over the hot chicken and egg mixture and garnish with the remaining spring onion. Serve immediately.

Kitsune Domburi
Rice with fried tofu

Serves: 6

Kitsune is the Japanese word for fox, and this dish is so named because, according to Japanese folklore, the fox has a great fondness for fried tofu which, with rice, is the chief ingredient in this dish.

4 sheets aburage (deep-fried tofu sheets)

625 ml (21 fl oz/2½ cups) Dashi (page 32) or Chicken stock (page 32)

125 ml (4 fl oz/½ cup) shoyu (Japanese soy sauce)

125 ml (4 fl oz/½ cup) mirin

1 tablespoon sugar

6 spring onions (scallions), thinly sliced diagonally

1 quantity cooked short-grain rice (page 17)

Put the aburage in a colander and pour over boiling water to make it less oily. Cut each aburage sheet in half lengthways, then cut widthways into thin strips.

Put the dashi, shoyu, mirin and sugar into a saucepan with the aburage and bring to the boil. Reduce the heat to low and simmer for 10 minutes, then add the spring onion, cover, and simmer for a further minute.

Put the rice into a large serving bowl or 6 individual bowls and ladle the hot soup over the top. Serve immediately.

Zaru Soba
Chilled noodles

Serves: 4

200 g (7 oz) soba noodles

1 sheet nori

1 tablespoon finely grated fresh ginger

3 spring onions (scallions), very thinly
sliced

Dipping sauce

500 ml (17 fl oz/2 cups) Dashi (page 32)

125 ml (4 fl oz/½ cup) shoyu
(Japanese soy sauce)

125 ml (4 fl oz/½ cup) mirin

salt or sugar to taste (optional)

To make the dipping sauce, put the dashi, shoyu and mirin into a small saucepan, stir to combine, and bring to the boil. Remove from the heat and cool. Taste, and add salt or sugar as desired. Set aside.

Bring a large saucepan of water to the boil and add the soba noodles. When the water returns to the boil, add 250 ml (8½ fl oz/1 cup) cold water. Bring to the boil again and cook for about 2 minutes, or until the noodles are just tender. Rinse under cold running water until they are quite cool. Drain well.

Toast the nori over an open flame or under a hot grill (broiler) until crisp. Put the noodles on plates and crumble the nori over the top. Mix together the ginger and spring onion and put a small portion on each plate. The ginger mixture is stirred into the dipping sauce and the noodles are dipped in the sauce before eating.

Sushi
Rice with vinegar and sugar

Serves: 6

Sushi is simply rice flavoured with a vinegar and sugar dressing and rolled around fillings or enclosed in omelettes or tofu.

550 g (1 lb 3 oz/2½ cups) short-grain rice

5 cm (2 in) piece kombu, rinsed and drained (optional)

Sushi dressing

80 ml (2½ fl oz/⅓ cup) rice vinegar or mild white vinegar

55 g (2 oz/¼ cup) sugar

2½ teaspoons salt

2 tablespoons mirin

Wash the rice well and drain in a colander for 30 minutes. Put the rice into a heavy-based saucepan with a tight-fitting lid, add 625 ml (21 fl oz/2½ cups) cold water and the kombu, if using. Bring to the boil, then reduce the heat to low, cover, and simmer for 15 minutes without lifting the lid. Remove from the heat and let the rice stand, still covered, for a further 10 minutes.

Meanwhile, make the dressing. Combine all the ingredients in a bowl and stir until the sugar is completely dissolved.

Discard the kombu and turn the rice out into a large bowl. Pour the dressing over the rice and mix gently but thoroughly and cool quickly to room temperature. Traditionally, this is done by fanning the rice as you turn it with a paddle, being careful not to damage the grains.

Fukusa Zushi
Sushi wrapped in omelette

Makes: about 8

½ quantity Chirashi-zushi (page 23)

4 eggs, lightly beaten

½ teaspoon salt

a few drops of sesame oil or vegetable oil for cooking

thin strips of dried nori

Press the chirashi-zushi firmly into a square or rectangular casserole dish or cake tin to a depth of 2.5 cm (1 in). Weight it down and leave while cooking the omelette.

Season the egg with the salt and stir in 2 tablespoons water. Cook the egg in a lightly oiled pan to make 8 thin omelettes. Cook over low heat and do not allow the omelettes to brown.

Cut the pressed sushi into eight 5 cm (2 in) square portions. Put a square of sushi in the centre of each omelette and roll up or fold over to enclose the rice. Wrap a thin strip of nori around each parcel and arrange on a serving plate, seam side down. Serve cold.

Inari-Zushi
Sushi in fried tofu

Makes: 12–16

In Japanese grocery stores you can buy sheets of aburage (deep-fried tofu). These form 'pockets', which are filled with sushi. Use half as many sheets of aburage as the number of inari-zushi you want, as each sheet makes two.

6–8 sheets of aburage (deep-fried tofu)

shoyu (Japanese soy sauce)

mirin or dry sherry

125 ml (4 fl oz/½ cup) Dashi (page 32) or Chicken stock (page 32) (optional)

1 tablespoon sugar

1 quantity Sushi (page 21)

Put the aburage in a colander and pour over boiling water to make it less oily. Press out most of the water by rolling in paper towel. Sprinkle a few drops of shoyu and mirin over each sheet to give it flavour. Alternatively, put the aburage in a saucepan with simmering dashi, 2 tablespoons shoyu, 1 tablespoon mirin and 1 tablespoon sugar until all the liquid has been absorbed by the tofu. Press out any excess moisture by rolling in paper towel.

Cut the aburage sheets in half and pull the sides apart to make a pocket. Spoon the sushi into each pocket so that it is three-quarters full, then fold the cut ends over to enclose the filling. Serve on a tray, folded side down.

Chirashi-Zushi
Rice with seafood and vegetables

Serves: 6

There are no hard and fast rules for making this Japanese version of a rice salad – add whatever ingredients are readily available for a colourful and easy main dish.

4 dried shiitake mushrooms

1 tablespoon shoyu (Japanese soy sauce)

1 teaspoon sugar

2 eggs, lightly beaten

a pinch of salt

vegetable oil for frying

1 quantity Sushi (page 21), cooled

85 g (3 oz/½ cup) cooked crabmeat or small chopped prawns (shrimp)

100 g (3½ oz/½ cup) thinly sliced sashimi-grade raw fish (optional)

160 g (5½ oz/⅔ cup) thinly sliced bamboo shoot

80 g (2¾ oz/½ cup) cooked peas

1 piece tinned or frozen lotus root, sliced

1 tablespoon pickled kombu, thinly sliced

1 tablespoon takuan (pickled daikon/ white radish), thinly sliced

pickled ginger (beni shoga) to garnish

Soak the mushrooms in hot water for 20–30 minutes. Drain, reserving 125 ml (4 fl oz/½ cup) of the soaking liquid, then cut off and discard the stems and thinly slice the caps.

Put the reserved soaking liquid into a saucepan with the shoyu and sugar. Add the mushroom and simmer for 10 minutes, or until the liquid has been absorbed.

Season the egg with the salt and cook in a lightly oiled pan to make a thin omelette, taking care not to let it brown. Cool, then cut into thin shreds.

Put the rice in a large bowl and toss gently with all the ingredients, reserving a few of the most colourful for garnish. Serve cold.

Nigiri Zushi
Rice with raw fish

Makes: about 24

1 quantity Sushi and dressing (page 21)

500 g (1 lb 2 oz) sashimi-grade tuna or salmon (see note)

2 teaspoons wasabi paste

pickled ginger (beni shoga) to serve

Note

Sashimi-grade tuna or salmon are prime cuts of very fresh fish. Snapper or bream (porgy) may be used if it is very fresh and has never been frozen. Sushi can also be made with cooked prawns (shrimp). You will need to peel and devein them and split them in half lengthways so they are butterflied before placing over the rice. If squid is used, cut the tubes into pieces just large enough to cover the mounds of rice. Blanch in boiling water for 1 minute. Drain, cool and place over the rice. Decorate with a strip of nori.

Prepare the rice according to the recipe on page 21 and reserve 2 tablespoons of the dressing, flavouring the sushi with the remainder.

Cut the fish into very thin slices with a sharp knife, angling the knife so that the slices are larger than they would be if cut straight. Cover with plastic wrap and refrigerate until needed.

In a bowl, combine the reserved sushi dressing with 2 tablespoons cold water and use it to moisten your hands before starting to shape the rice. Take a rounded tablespoon of sushi at a time and form each into a neat oval shape. They should be a little smaller than the slices of fish, so that the fish completely covers one side of the rice.

In a bowl, combine the wasabi paste with 2 teaspoons cold water to make a dressing. Spread each slice of fish with a little wasabi dressing and put it, dressing side down, on the rice. Mould to a neat shape. Repeat with the remaining rice and fish. Arrange on a tray and serve garnished with the pickled ginger.

Norimaki Zushi
Sushi rolled in seaweed

Makes: about 36

4 dried shiitake mushrooms

2 tablespoons shoyu (Japanese soy sauce)

1 tablespoon sugar

2 eggs, lightly beaten

¼ teaspoon salt

a few drops of sesame oil or vegetable oil
for cooking

1 telegraph (long) cucumber

1 small piece takuan (pickled daikon/
white radish)

125 g (4½ oz) sashimi-grade fish fillets,
such as tuna, bonito or kingfish

1 teaspoon wasabi paste

6 sheets nori

1 quantity Sushi (page 21)

Soak the mushrooms in hot water for 20–30 minutes. Drain, reserving 125 ml (4 fl oz/½ cup) of the soaking liquid, then cut off and discard the stems and thinly slice the caps. Put the reserved soaking liquid into a saucepan with the shoyu and sugar. Add the mushroom and simmer for 10 minutes, or until the liquid has been absorbed.

Season the egg with the salt and cook in a lightly oiled pan to make a thin omelette, taking care not to let it brown. Cool, then cut into thin shreds.

Peel the cucumber leaving a trace of green skin. Cut lengthways in strips the size of a pencil. Drain the pickled daikon and cut in similar-sized strips. Cut the fish in strips and smear with the wasabi.

Toast the nori sheets over an open flame or place under a hot grill (broiler) until crisp. Put a sheet of nori on a bamboo sushi mat, or on a clean linen napkin. Divide the rice into 6 equal portions and spread one portion evenly over two-thirds of each nori sheet, starting at the end nearest you. In a row across the middle of the rice put one of the ingredients or a combination of ingredients. Roll up the sushi in the mat, keeping firm pressure on the rice so that a neatly packed cylinder results. Let the rolls rest for 10 minutes before cutting into about 6 pieces per roll. Arrange on a platter with extra wasabi, pickled ginger and soy sauce to accompany.

Uramaki
California rolls

Makes: about 8

This is an inside out sushi roll – the seaweed, which encloses a filling, is wrapped in rice then coated with caviar. I think I like flying fish roe (tobiko) best for its resilient crunch. The tiny eggs literally pop between the teeth. It comes in a choice of colours – orange (natural) and green (wasabi) are the most popular.

8–10 sheets nori

1 quantity Sushi with 2 tablespoons Sushi dressing (page 21)

2 ripe but firm avocados

265 g (9½ oz/1½ cups) crabmeat

Japanese mayonnaise

125 g (4½ oz) caviar, preferably flying fish roe (tobiko)

Cover a bamboo mat with plastic wrap to minimise sticking.

Toast the nori sheets over an open flame or place under a hot grill (broiler) until crisp. Lay a sheet of nori on the bamboo mat and cover with a thin layer of sushi rice. To do this most efficiently, wet your hands first so that the rice doesn't stick to them and spread evenly with your fingers, without mashing the grains. Flip the seaweed over, rice side down, on the mat.

Arrange slices of avocado lengthways along the centre of the nori. Squeeze a little Japanese mayonnaise in a line alongside the avocado and top with the crabmeat. Roll up, starting at the edge nearest you, by lifting the mat to get it started and continue rolling away from you, peeling back the mat as you go. Coat the finished roll in caviar, pressing it on firmly until it sticks to the rice. Cut each roll into slices to reveal the contrasting colours. Serve cold.

Snacks,
Starters and
Soups

Gyoza
Fried and steamed dumplings

Serves: 6

6 dried shiitake mushrooms

225 g (8 oz/3 cups) shredded Chinese cabbage (wombok)

½ teaspoon salt

350 g (12½ oz) minced (ground) pork

1 teaspoon grated fresh ginger

6 spring onions (scallions), thinly sliced

1 tablespoon finely chopped coriander (cilantro) leaves

2 teaspoons miso paste

1 teaspoon sesame oil, plus 1 tablespoon extra

½ teaspoon dried chilli flakes or ⅛ teaspoon chilli powder

¼ teaspoon sugar

48 round gyoza wrappers

Chilli dipping sauce (below) or Ponzu sauce (page 30) to serve

Soak the mushrooms in hot water for 20–30 minutes. Drain, reserving 125 ml (4 fl oz/½ cup) of the soaking liquid, then cut off and discard the stems and thinly slice the caps.

Put the cabbage and salt in a large bowl and leave for 15 minutes. Squeeze out any excess liquid by hand, then place in a large bowl with the pork, mushroom, ginger, spring onion, coriander, miso, sesame oil, chilli and sugar. Knead well until thoroughly mixed.

Lay the wrappers out on a clean work surface and place a rounded teaspoon in the centre of each. Moisten the edges, fold over and pinch and pleat to enclose the filling, working from the centre out so they resemble a crescent-shaped pouch. Set aside on a tray lined with baking paper. Repeat until all are used.

Heat a little sesame oil in the base of a large heavy-based frying pan over medium heat. Fry the dumplings, pleat side up, in batches, until brown on the base, until all are cooked.

Return the dumplings to the pan so they are close but not touching, add the remaining sesame oil and reserved soaking liquid, cover, and steam over low heat for about 10 minutes, or until the wrappers become semi-transparent. Remove the lid and continue cooking until all the liquid has been absorbed, shaking the pan as needed to prevent the dumplings from sticking. Serve hot with chilli dipping sauce or ponzu sauce.

Chilli Dipping Sauce

100 ml (3½ fl oz) shoyu (Japanese soy sauce)

60 ml (2 fl oz/¼ cup) rice vinegar

½ teaspoon sugar (optional)

½ teaspoon sesame oil

a few drops of chilli oil, or to taste

Combine all the ingredients in a bowl, stirring to dissolve the sugar, if using. Serve with Gyoza (above).

Snacks, Starters and Soups ✦

Beef Tataki With Ponzu Sauce
Rare seared beef

Serves: 4

This beef dish is served cold as an appetiser. Sashimi-grade tuna fillet can be used instead of the beef but it will need to be seared very briefly before serving.

250 g (9 oz) porterhouse steak, about 5 cm
(2 in) thick

1 tablespoon light olive oil

3 spring onions (scallions), very
thinly sliced

Ponzu sauce

125 ml (4 fl oz/½ cup) shoyu (Japanese
soy sauce)

6 g (¼ oz/½ cup) bonito flakes
(katsuobushi)

1 tablespoon mirin

60 ml (2 fl oz/¼ cup) lemon juice

Put the steak in a bowl, pour over the oil and turn to coat all over. Heat a cast-iron frying pan over high heat and when very hot place the steak in the pan and cook for 1½–2 minutes – do not turn during this time. Once the time is up, turn it and cook for a further 1–2 minutes – the meat will be very rare. Remove to a plate and allow to cool completely.

To make the ponzu sauce, put the shoyu in a stainless steel saucepan and bring to the boil. Add the bonito flakes, then turn off the heat and leave to cool. Add the mirin and lemon juice and then strain into an airtight jar and refrigerate until ready to use. Ponzu sauce can be stored for up to 10 days.

Place the steak on a board, trim away any sinew, then cut into thin slices, about 2 mm (⅛ in) thick. Arrange on a serving platter so that the slices just overlap. Scatter over the spring onion and about 80 ml (2½ fl oz/⅓ cup) of the ponzu sauce.

Variation

To be completely authentic, use yuzu juice to make the ponzu sauce instead of lemon juice. This Japanese citrus is not yet available fresh in Australia, and the bottled juice is both hard to find and prohibitively expensive. A combination of lemon juice, lime juice and a little grapefruit juice also makes a very acceptable substitute.

Dashi
Dashi stock

Makes: 1.5 litres (51 fl oz/6 cups)

Dashi is basic to Japanese cooking and is quickly and easily made. It may be kept refrigerated for up to 2 days, so if you have surplus, freeze it. Even simpler to prepare (and useful to have on hand) is instant dashi, sold in packets.

5 cm (2 in) square kombu, rinsed and drained

3 tablespoons bonito flakes (katsuobushi)

Put 1.5 litres (51 fl oz/6 cups) water in a saucepan and bring to the boil. Stir in the kombu and boil for 1 minute, then remove the kombu from the water and add the bonito flakes. Bring back to the boil, then remove from the heat immediately. Leave for a few minutes until the flakes settle, then strain and use as required.

Chicken stock

Makes: 1.5 litres (51 fl oz/6 cups)

When a different flavour is preferred, or if ingredients for dashi cannot be obtained, use this Japanese-style chicken stock in place of the more traditional dashi.

1 kg (2 lb 3 oz) chicken bones or carcass

3–4 large slices fresh ginger

1½ teaspoons salt

2 spring onions (scallions)

Put the chicken bones into a large saucepan with all the other ingredients and 2 litres (68 fl oz/8 cups) water and bring to the boil. Reduce the heat to low, cover, and simmer for about 1 hour, skimming to remove any scum from the surface. Remove from the heat, then strain into a clean bowl or saucepan. Chill so that any fat solidifies on the surface and can be removed before using – the stock should be very clear.

Sakana Ushiojiru
Fish broth

Serves: 4

500 g (1 lb 2 oz) bones, head and trimmings of any delicate fish

2 slices fresh ginger

1 spring onion (scallion), cut into 4 pieces, plus 1 tablespoon thinly sliced spring onion, extra

1 tablespoon shoyu (Japanese soy sauce)

1 tablespoon sake

4 slices raw fish (optional)

Put the fish bones, head and trimmings into a saucepan with 1.5 litres (51 fl oz/6 cups) water, the ginger and spring onion. Bring to the boil, then reduce the heat to low and simmer for about 10–15 minutes, skimming off any scum that rises to the surface. Remove from the heat, allow to cool slightly and then strain into a clean pan. Stir in the shoyu, sake and salt, to taste.

To serve, heat the soup to boiling and stir in the extra spring onion. Remove from the heat immediately and serve. If liked, a thin slice of raw fish can be put in each bowl and the boiling broth ladled over.

Kakejiru
Soup for noodles

Makes: 1.75 litres (60 fl oz/7 cups)

This is the basic stock in which noodles of all kinds may be served. If preferred, clear chicken stock may be substituted for the dashi.

1.5 litres (51 fl oz/6 cups) Dashi (opposite)

125 ml (4 fl oz/½ cup) mirin

125 ml (4 fl oz/½ cup) shoyu (Japanese soy sauce)

Put the dashi, mirin and shoyu into a saucepan and bring to the boil. Reduce the heat to low, cover, and simmer for 10 minutes. Taste and add extra salt if necessary.

Miso Shiru
Bean paste soup

Serves: 4

1.25 litres (42 fl oz/5 cups) Dashi (page 32)

2 tablespoons miso paste

100 g (3½ oz) silken tofu, cut into quarters

2 spring onions (scallions), sliced diagonally

2 fresh shiitake or button mushrooms, sliced

Put the dashi into a saucepan and bring to the boil.

In a bowl, combine the miso with some of the hot liquid, stirring until smooth. Pour the mixture back into the saucepan, stir well, then add the tofu and spring onion and return to the boil for a few seconds only. Ladle the soup into bowls, garnish with mushroom slices and serve hot.

Sumashi Wan
Prawn and tofu soup

Serves: 6

1 small carrot

1.5 litres (51 fl oz/6 cups) Dashi (page 32)

6 raw prawns (shrimp), peeled and deveined

100 g (3½ oz) silken tofu, sliced

watercress sprigs to garnish

Peel the carrot and cut off both ends so you are left with a straight cross-section. With a sharp cleaver remove narrow V-shaped strips the length of the carrot at regular intervals, then slice across very thinly to make flower shapes. Drop into boiling water for 1 minute, then drain and refresh in iced water. Set aside for garnish.

Put the dashi into a saucepan and bring to the boil. Add the prawns and simmer for 1 minute, then add the tofu and bring back to the boil. Remove from the heat and ladle carefully into soup bowls, putting a prawn and a slice of tofu in each bowl. Fill the bowls with stock, then garnish each with a sprig of watercress and one or two carrot slices. Serve immediately.

Kakitama-Jiru
Egg flower soup

Serves: 4

Poetically named for the texture the beaten egg takes on as it sets in the boiling stock.

1.25 litres (42 fl oz/5 cups) Dashi (page 32)
   or Chicken stock (page 32)

8 snow peas (mangetout), trimmed or
   1 celery stalk, sliced

2 tablespoons shoyu (Japanese soy sauce)

2 eggs, lightly beaten

½ teaspoon salt

Put the dashi in a saucepan and bring to the boil. Add the snow peas and once the liquid returns to the boil, cook for 1 minute, then add the shoyu.

Season the egg with the salt and pour slowly into the boiling stock, stirring gently so it sets in shreds. Ladle into soup bowls and serve immediately.

Dashimaki Tamago
Rolled omelette

Serves: 4

Japanese omelette pans are rectangular. If you can get one it will make your rolled omelettes easier to handle and neater in appearance, but a regular frying pan can be used quite successfully.

2 teaspoons sugar

¼ teaspoon salt

125 ml (4 fl oz/½ cup) Dashi (page 32)

2 teaspoons shoyu (Japanese soy sauce)

5 eggs, lightly beaten

sesame oil for cooking

parsley sprigs to garnish

In a bowl, dissolve the sugar and salt in the dashi, then stir in the shoyu and egg.

Heat a few drops of oil in an omelette pan over low heat. Pour in one-third of the egg mixture and tilt the pan so the egg covers the base. Cook until just set – the omelette must not brown. Once cooked, keep the omelette in the pan and roll it away from you. When the omelette is completely rolled up, lightly grease the pan again, slide the omelette towards you and grease that part of the pan where the omelette was. Pour in half the remaining egg mixture and lift the egg roll so the uncooked egg can cover the base of the pan. Cook as before and roll again, this time rolling the first omelette within the second one.

Repeat as before, using the remaining beaten egg. Turn the omelette onto a bamboo mat or a clean tea towel (dish towel) and roll the omelette firmly. Leave it for 10 minutes to cool and compress, then remove the mat and cut the rolled egg into thick slices. Serve garnished with the parsley.

Nabeyaki Udon
Hearty noodle soup

Serves: 6

6 dried shiitake mushrooms

500 g (1 lb 2 oz) udon noodles

1.5 litres (6 cups) Kakejiru (soup for noodles) (page 33)

1 large boneless skinless chicken breast, thinly sliced

1 Japanese-style fish cake (kamaboko), sliced

12 cooked large prawns (shrimp), peeled and deveined, tails left intact, to garnish

2 spring onions (scallions), thinly sliced diagonally

Soak the mushrooms in hot water for 20–30 minutes. Drain, then cut off and discard the stems and thinly slice the caps.

Bring a large saucepan of water to the boil and add the udon noodles. When the water returns to the boil add 250 ml (8½ fl oz/1 cup) cold water. Bring to the boil again and cook until the udon noodles are just tender, being careful not to overcook. Rinse under cold running water to cool them and drain well.

Put the kakejiru in a saucepan and bring to the boil. Add the mushroom and chicken and simmer for 3 minutes, then add the noodles and heat through. Add the fish cake, prawns and spring onion, cover, and simmer for a further 1–2 minutes for the prawns to heat through. Serve immediately.

Kenchin-Jiru (1)
Chicken and vegetable soup

Serves: 6

4 dried shiitake mushrooms

1.75 litres (60 fl oz/7 cups) Dashi (page 32) or Chicken stock (page 32)

1 small carrot, cut into thin matchsticks

1 celery stalk, cut into thin matchsticks

½ large daikon (white radish), cut into thin matchsticks

200 g (7 oz) boneless skinless chicken breasts or thighs, diced

Soak the mushrooms in hot water for 20–30 minutes. Drain, then cut off and discard the stems and thinly slice the caps.

Put the mushroom and dashi into a saucepan and bring to the boil, then reduce the heat to low, cover, and simmer for 10 minutes. Add the carrot, celery, daikon and chicken and cook for 5 minutes. Taste and season with salt, to taste. Serve hot.

Kenchin-Jiru (2)
Chicken and vegetable soup

Serves: 6

More suited to Western tastes than the previous recipe, this version of kenchin-jiru is based on chicken stock and uses button mushrooms instead of shiitake. Any thick stalks from the watercress may be added to the simmering stock and strained off before serving.

1.5 litres (51 fl oz/6 cups) Chicken stock (page 32)

1 small boneless skinless chicken breast, diced

125 g (4½ oz) button mushrooms, sliced if large

1 spring onion (scallion), cut into short lengths

a few watercress sprigs to garnish

Put the chicken stock into a saucepan and bring to the boil, then reduce the heat, add the chicken and simmer for about 3 minutes. Add the mushrooms and spring onion to the pan and bring back to the boil. Remove from the heat, divide among soup bowls and garnish with the watercress sprigs.

Seafood

❖

Saba No Sutataki
Mackerel in vinegar marinade

Serves: 4

500 g (1 lb 2 oz) mackerel fillets

salt

125 ml (4 fl oz/½ cup) mild white vinegar

2 tablespoons sugar

4 tablespoons finely grated daikon
  (white radish)

4 tablespoons finely grated carrot

watercress or parsley sprigs to garnish

wasabi paste to serve

Dipping sauce

1 teaspoon finely grated fresh ginger

60 ml (2 fl oz/¼ cup) shoyu
  (Japanese soy sauce)

2 tablespoons mild white vinegar

1 tablespoon sugar

Rub the mackerel fillets liberally with salt and refrigerate for at least 3 hours or overnight.

Remove any bones, rinse off any excess salt, then thinly slice the fish.

In a bowl, combine the vinegar, sugar and 2 tablespoons cold water, then add to the fish and toss to coat. Leave to marinate for 30 minutes.

Arrange the fish slices on individual plates, put a tablespoon each of grated daikon and carrot on each plate and garnish with watercress or parsley.

To make the dipping sauce, combine the ginger, shoyu, vinegar and sugar in a bowl, stirring well. Serve the fish and vegetables with small bowls of the dipping sauce and wasabi.

Sakana No Gingami Yaki
Seafood and vegetables in foil

Serves: 4

4 dried shiitake mushrooms

4 firm white fish fillets

½ teaspoon salt

1 tablespoon sake

8 raw large prawns (shrimp)

12 ginkgo nuts

Soak the mushrooms in hot water for 20–30 minutes. Drain, then cut off and discard the stems and thinly slice the caps. Preheat the oven to 170°C (340°F).

Wipe the fish with damp paper towel. Sprinkle the salt over the fish, pour over the sake and leave to marinate for 10 minutes.

Remove the prawn heads and cut along the back of the shell with a sharp knife so that the vein can be removed without peeling the prawn.

Take pieces of foil, about 25 cm (10 in) square, and lightly oil one side. Put a fish fillet, 2 prawns, some mushroom and 3 ginkgo nuts on each square of foil. Fold the foil to form a parcel and bake in the oven for 20 minutes, or cook over coals on a barbecue or under a hot grill (broiler). Serve hot in the foil parcel.

Seafood

Sashimi
Raw fish

Serves: 1

Use only the freshest seafood for this Japanese delicacy. Buy whole fish or sashimi-grade fillets. Far from being strong or fishy, the flavour is indescribably delicate. Wasabi is served with the fish and each person mixes some with soy sauce for dipping the fish in before eating.

For each serving

125 g (4½ oz) sashimi-grade tuna or salmon fillets, or very fresh whole bonito, mackerel, jewfish or squid

1 tablespoon grated daikon (white radish)

1 tablespoon grated carrot

shiso leaves or watercress sprigs to serve (optional)

lemon slices to serve

1 teaspoon wasabi paste

shoyu (Japanese soy sauce) to serve

mirin or dry sherry to serve

If using whole fish, fillet the fish, removing all bones. Carefully cut away the skin. With a sharp knife, and handling the fish as little as possible, cut the fillet into thin slices and arrange on a serving plate. Tuna and bonito are suitable for cutting into small cubes; cut small fish or squid into thin strips.

Serve the fish with the daikon and carrot, decorate the plate with a shiso leaf or a watercress sprig and a slice of lemon or yuzu, if you can get it. Accompany each serving with a dab of wasabi and a sauce dish holding shoyu or a mixture of shoyu and mirin.

Kinome Yaki
Grilled marinated fish

Serves: 4

2 large oily fish steaks, such as tuna or
mackerel

80 ml (2½ fl oz/⅓ cup) shoyu
(Japanese soy sauce)

2 tablespoons mirin

2 tablespoons sake

2 teaspoons finely grated fresh ginger

1 tablespoon sugar

Garnish

pickled ginger (beni shoga), spring onions
(scallions) or cucumber, thinly sliced

60 ml (2 fl oz/¼ cup) white vinegar

55 g (2 oz/¼ cup) sugar

1 teaspoon shoyu (Japanese soy sauce)

1 teaspoon salt

Wipe the fish with damp paper towel. Cut each fish steak
into 4 even-sized pieces.

In a bowl, combine the shoyu, mirin and sake. Squeeze the
juice from the fresh ginger into this mixture, discarding the
fibres. Add the sugar and stir to dissolve. Add the fish and
leave to marinate for about 30 minutes.

Prepare the garnish by combining the vinegar, sugar, shoyu
and salt in a bowl. Add the ginger, spring onion or cucumber
and leave to marinate while cooking the fish.

Preheat the grill (broiler) and cook the fish about 10 cm
(4 in) away from the heat source for 5–7 minutes, brushing
2 or 3 times with the marinade. Turn the fish and grill the
other side – the fish should have a rich glaze of marinade.
Serve immediately with the prepared garnish.

Harusame Tempura
Deep-fried seafood

Serves: 4

....

Harusame are fine, translucent noodles, the Japanese equivalent of cellophane (bean thread) noodles. In this version of tempura, the ingredients are dipped first in cornflour (cornstarch), then in egg white and finally in harusame noodles snipped into small pieces. When deep-fried, the noodles expand in spectacular fashion and form a crisp coating for the seafood, making an eye-catching as well as tasty appetiser.

....

500 g (1 lb 2 oz) boneless, skinless firm, white fish fillets

1 tablespoon shoyu (Japanese soy sauce)

1 tablespoon mirin

½ teaspoon salt

12 raw prawns (shrimp), peeled and deveined, tails left intact

vegetable oil for deep-frying

60 g (2 oz/½ cup) cornflour (cornstarch)

2 egg whites, beaten until frothy

1½ cups finely snipped harusame noodles (they should be no more than 1 cm/½ in long)

Tempura sauce (page 46) or salt for dipping

Wipe the fish with damp paper towel. Cut each fillet lengthways into narrow strips, then into bite-sized lengths.

In a bowl, combine the shoyu, mirin and salt. Add the fish and prawns and leave to marinate for 30 minutes.

Heat the vegetable oil in a large heavy-based frying pan to about 180°C (350°F), or until a cube of bread dropped into the oil turns brown in 15 seconds. Roll each piece of seafood first in cornflour, dusting off any excess, then in egg white, then in harusame noodles to coat. Lower the seafood into the hot oil and deep-fry, in batches, for about 1 minute, or until crisp. The noodles will puff and swell immediately on being immersed in the hot oil; if they do not, it means the oil is not hot enough and the harusame will be tough and leathery. Remove from the oil using a slotted spoon and drain on paper towel. Serve hot with the tempura sauce or sea salt for dipping.

Tempura
Deep-fried seafood and vegetables

Serves: 4

....

Perhaps the most popular of all Japanese dishes among Western people, good tempura should be crisp and light; the batter a mere wisp that covers the food. It should never be the heavy coating found on traditional English-style fried fish (as in 'fish and chips'). A Japanese chef told me that the secret is to have both food and batter very cold and that the batter must be freshly made and not allowed to stand for too long. Tempura is best served the moment it is ready, so cooking at the table in an electric frying pan or deep-fryer is particularly suitable.

....

12–16 raw prawns (shrimp), peeled and deveined, tails left intact

500 g (1 lb 2 oz) boneless, skinless, firm, white fish fillets

350 g (12½ oz) frozen lotus root, peeled and thinly sliced

1 eggplant (aubergine), halved and cut into 5 mm (¼ in) slices

1 sweet potato, peeled and cut into 5 mm (¼ in) slices

90 g (3 oz/2 cups) baby English spinach leaves

8 spring onions (scallions), cut into short lengths

250 g (9 oz) fresh mushrooms, halved or quartered if large

4 tablespoons grated daikon (white radish) to serve

2 tablespoons finely grated fresh ginger to serve

750 ml (25½ fl oz/3 cups) vegetable oil

125 ml (4 fl oz/½ cup) sesame oil

Tempura batter

1 egg

250 ml (8½ fl oz/1 cup) ice-cold water

a pinch of bicarbonate of soda (baking soda)

110 g (4 oz/¾ cup) plain (all-purpose) flour or tempura flour

Tempura sauce

60 ml (2 fl oz/¼ cup) mirin

2 tablespoons shoyu (Japanese soy sauce)

250 ml (8½ fl oz/1 cup) Dashi (page 32)

a pinch of salt

Prepare the prawns, fish and all the vegetables in advance. Arrange on a tray, cover, and refrigerate until serving time.

The table setting for each person is a plate lined with a paper napkin for draining the fried food, a small bowl for the sauce and another small bowl with 1 tablespoon of grated daikon and 2 teaspoons of grated fresh ginger.

To make the tempura sauce, heat the mirin in a small saucepan, remove from the heat and ignite with a match. Shake the pan gently until the flame dies, then add all the other ingredients and bring to the boil. Remove from the heat and allow to cool to room temperature, taste, and adjust the seasoning if necessary. Set aside.

No more than 10 minutes before serving, make the tempura batter and stand the bowl in a larger bowl containing ice. Break the egg into a bowl with the iced water and beat until frothy. Add the bicarbonate of soda and flour and beat just until the flour is mixed in – do not overmix. The batter should be thin; if it seems too thick, add a few drops of iced water.

Heat the vegetable and sesame oils in a large heavy-based frying pan, electric frying pan or deep-fryer to 180°C (350°F), or until a cube of bread dropped into the oil turns brown in 15 seconds. If sesame oil is not available it may be omitted, but it gives a deliciously nutty flavour to the food.

Dip pieces of fish, prawns and vegetables, one at a time, into the batter and then gently lower into the oil. Do not fry more than about 6 pieces at a time, as the temperature of the oil must be kept moderately high for best results. As each piece turns golden (this should take only 1 minute) lift it from the oil with a slotted spoon, drain for a few seconds on paper towel, then serve immediately. Food is dipped in the tempura sauce and eaten while crisp and hot. The daikon and ginger are mixed into the sauce to suit individual taste.

Variation
A good way to use up any left-over tempura ingredients is to make tempura domburi (tendon), where the tempura ingredients are served with rice and sauce. Prepare 1 quantity hot cooked rice (see page 17) and re-fry the tempura briefly to heat through. Put the rice in individual bowls, top with the tempura and serve with any left-over sauce on the side.

Yosenabe
Simmered seafood and vegetables

Serves: 6

Other varieties of fish or vegetables as available may be substituted for those in this recipe.

500 g (1 lb 2 oz) snapper or bream (porgy) fillets

1 lobster tail

60 g (2 oz) cellophane (bean thread) noodles

2 litres (68 fl oz/8 cups) Dashi (page 32) or Chicken stock (page 32)

2 carrots, sliced

1 small piece kombu (optional)

shoyu (Japanese soy sauce) to taste

a few baby English spinach leaves

6 fresh shiitake or button mushrooms, sliced

6 spring onions (scallions), cut into short lengths

Wipe the fish with damp paper towel. Cut the fish into 2.5 cm (1 in) pieces. With a sharp cleaver, cut the lobster tail into slices, then cut each large slice into halves.

Soak the noodles in hot water for 20 minutes, then drain well and cut into short lengths. Put the noodles into a saucepan with the dashi, bring to the boil, then reduce the heat to low and simmer for 5 minutes. Add the carrot, kombu and shoyu and continue simmering for a further 2 minutes. Add the fish, lobster, spinach, mushroom and spring onion and continue to simmer for 5 minutes or until everything is just cooked. Serve in soup bowls accompanied by small dishes of dipping sauce as served with Zaru soba (page 20).

Chawan Mushi
Steamed egg custard with seafood

Serves: 4

This savoury egg custard is regarded as a soup in Japan and is ideal as a light lunch or supper dish. If you want to make a single portion, beat the egg in the cup in which it will be cooked (Japanese cooks use chopsticks for this), pour in stock to three-quarters fill the cup and add salt, shoyu (Japanese soy sauce) and sake, to taste. Add other ingredients as available – it's a good way to use up a few prawns (shrimp) or oysters. In summer these custard soups may be served cold. They are the only soups that are eaten with a spoon.

4 dried shiitake mushrooms

2 tablespoons shoyu (Japanese soy sauce)

1 tablespoon sugar

4 fresh oysters or 4 thin slices fresh tuna

4 small prawns (shrimp), peeled and deveined or 8 slices Japanese-style fish cake (kamaboko)

Custard

4 eggs

625 ml (21 fl oz/2½ cups) Dashi (page 32)

1½ teaspoons salt

1 tablespoon shoyu (Japanese soy sauce)

2 tablespoons sake or mirin

Note

If preferred, substitute thinly sliced chicken breast for the seafood. You will need 1 small boneless skinless chicken breast for this quantity.

Soak the mushrooms in hot water for 20–30 minutes. Drain, reserving 125 ml (4 fl oz/½ cup) of the soaking liquid, then cut off and discard the stems.

Put the mushroom caps in a small saucepan with the reserved soaking liquid, 1 tablespoon of the shoyu and the sugar and simmer for 8–10 minutes. If tuna is used, marinate for a few minutes in the remaining tablespoon of shoyu.

Into each of 4 *chawan mushi* cups or 250 ml (8½ fl oz/1 cup) capacity ramekins, put a mushroom, a prawn or 2 slices of fish cake, an oyster or a slice of marinated tuna.

To make the custard, lightly beat the eggs just until the whites and yolks are mixed. Stir in the dashi, salt, shoyu and sake, then strain the custard and pour into the cups. Cover with lids or foil.

Put the cups in a large saucepan and pour in enough water to come halfway up the sides of the cups. Cover the pan with a folded tea towel (dish towel) and then with the lid. Bring to the boil, then reduce the heat to low and simmer for 15 minutes, or until set. Alternatively, place the cups in a large baking tray and fill the tray with water to come halfway up the sides of the cups. Cook in a 160°C (320°F) oven for 25 minutes. Serve hot.

Meat

Oboro
Rice with chicken and mushrooms

Serves: 6

....

8 dried shiitake mushrooms

2 eggs, lightly beaten

⅛ teaspoon salt

80 ml (2½ fl oz/⅓ cup) shoyu
  (Japanese soy sauce)

80 ml (2½ fl oz/⅓ cup) mirin

2 tablespoons sugar

375 g (13 oz) boneless skinless chicken
  breast, thinly sliced

1 quantity cooked rice (page 17) to serve

140 g (5 oz/1 cup) cooked green peas
  to serve

Soak the mushrooms in hot water for 20–30 minutes. Drain, reserving 190 ml (6½ fl oz/¾ cup) of the soaking liquid, then cut off and discard the stems.

Season the egg with the salt and cook in a lightly greased frying pan to make 2 or 3 large, thin omelettes, taking care not to brown them. Remove to a plate and when cool cut into fine strips. Set aside.

Put the mushrooms in a small saucepan with 125 ml (4 fl oz/½ cup) of the reserved soaking liquid, 2 tablespoons each of the shoyu and mirin, and 1 tablespoon of the sugar. Bring to the boil, cover, and cook until the liquid is almost completely evaporated. Remove the mushrooms to a plate and allow to cool.

Add the remaining shoyu, mirin and sugar to the same pan, then add the remaining mushroom soaking liquid and the chicken and bring to the boil. Reduce the heat to low, cover, and simmer for 3 minutes. Turn off the heat and leave covered.

Spoon the hot rice into a large domburi or earthenware bowl with a lid, arrange the chicken over the top and spoon over the cooking liquid. Slice the mushrooms and scatter over the chicken, then garnish with the omelette strips and peas and serve hot.

Meat

Torimaki
Chicken omelette

Serves: 2

---

3 eggs, lightly beaten

2 tablespoons Dashi (page 32) or water

½ teaspoon salt

1 teaspoon shoyu (Japanese soy sauce)

vegetable or sesame oil for frying

2 spring onions (scallions), thinly sliced into strips, to garnish

Chicken filling

90 g (3 oz/½ cup) finely chopped cooked chicken

2 teaspoons shoyu (Japanese soy sauce)

2 teaspoons mirin

1 teaspoon sugar

1 teaspoon finely grated fresh ginger

In a bowl, combine the egg, dashi, salt and shoyu and stir to combine.

To make the chicken filling, put the chicken, shoyu, mirin and sugar into a separate bowl. Squeeze in the juice from the ginger, discarding the fibres. Stir well to combine.

Heat a few drops of the oil in an omelette pan over low heat. Pour in the egg and cook until set on the bottom, but liquid on top. Put the chicken filling in a neat line across the omelette and roll the egg mixture firmly around it, away from you. Remove to a plate and serve immediately, garnished with spring onion.

Note

This chicken omelette may also be rolled in a bamboo mat, left until cool and firm, then unrolled, sliced and served as an hors d'oeuvre.

Tatsuta Age
Marinated fried chicken

Serves: 4

....

500 g (1 lb 2 oz) boneless skinless chicken
   thighs

60 ml (2 fl oz/¼ cup) shoyu
   (Japanese soy sauce)

2 tablespoons sake

2 teaspoons sugar

60 g (2 oz/½ cup) cornflour (cornstarch)

oil for deep frying

Cut the chicken into bite-sized pieces.

In a bowl, combine the shoyu, sake and sugar. Add the chicken, toss to coat and leave to marinate for at least 1 hour.

Drain the chicken, then roll each piece in cornflour to coat and set aside for 10 minutes.

Heat the oil in a frying pan to 180°C (350°F), or until a cube of bread dropped into the oil turns brown in 15 seconds, and deep-fry the chicken, in batches, for about 2–3 minutes, or until golden brown and crisp. Drain on paper towel and serve hot.

Goma Yaki
Fried chicken with sesame

Serves: 4

....

1 tablespoon sesame seeds

4 boneless chicken breasts, preferably with
   skin on

80 ml (2½ fl oz/⅓ cup) sake

1 teaspoon salt

1 teaspoon shoyu (Japanese soy sauce)

1 tablespoon sesame oil

4 crisp lettuce leaves

Toast the sesame seeds in a dry frying pan over medium heat, stirring constantly, until they are golden. Remove to a plate to cool.

In a bowl, combine the sake, salt and shoyu. Prick the skin of the chicken several times with a skewer. Add the chicken and turn to coat both sides, then set aside for 30 minutes.

Heat the sesame oil in a frying pan over medium heat. Add the chicken and cook until brown on both sides. Reduce the heat and cook for 4–5 minutes, or until cooked through. Cut each chicken breast into slices and put back together in shape. Sprinkle with the sesame seeds and serve each chicken breast on a lettuce leaf.

Yakitori Domburi
Rice with fried chicken

Serves: 6

1.2 kg (2 lb 10 oz) whole chicken

125 ml (4 fl oz/½ cup) shoyu
   (Japanese soy sauce)

125 ml (4 fl oz/½ cup) mirin

2 garlic cloves, crushed

1 teaspoon finely grated fresh ginger

60 ml (2 fl oz/¼ cup) vegetable oil

3 teaspoons sugar

3 spring onions (scallions), thinly sliced

1 quantity cooked rice (page 17) to serve

Joint the chicken (see page 10) and cut into serving pieces.

In a bowl, combine the shoyu, mirin, garlic and ginger. Add the chicken, reserving the chicken back and wing tips to make a stock. Turn to coat the chicken and leave to marinate for 30 minutes.

Put the chicken back and wing tips in a saucepan with enough water to cover and bring to the boil. Reduce the heat to low and simmer for 2 hours. Strain the stock into a clean saucepan – you should be left with about 750 ml (25½ fl oz/3 cups) stock.

Drain the chicken well, reserving the marinade. Heat the vegetable oil in a large heavy-based frying pan over medium heat. Add the chicken and cook until golden brown. Remove from the heat and allow to cool slightly, then cut the meat into bite-sized pieces.

Add the reserved marinade and sugar to the pan with the stock, bring to the boil and cook for 2 minutes. Stir in the spring onion to combine, then remove from the heat. Arrange the hot cooked rice in a large bowl or individual bowls and arrange the chicken on top. Pour the sauce over the rice and chicken and serve immediately.

Tori Teriyaki
Grilled marinated chicken

Serves: 6

1.5 kg (3 lb 5 oz) whole chicken

125 ml (4 fl oz/½ cup) shoyu
   (Japanese soy sauce)

125 ml (4 fl oz/½ cup) mirin

2 tablespoons sugar

1 garlic clove, crushed with a pinch of salt

1½ teaspoons finely grated fresh ginger

a few drops of sesame oil or vegetable oil

Note

To cook chicken teriyaki in a frying pan, drain the pieces of chicken well, reserving the marinade. Dry the chicken on paper towel and pierce the skin a few times with a fork. Heat 2 tablespoons oil in a large heavy-based frying pan and cook the chicken, skin side down first, then turning until brown on both sides. Drain off the oil, add half the marinade to the pan, reduce the heat to low, cover, and cook for 15–20 minutes, or until the chicken is almost tender. Uncover and cook for a further 5 minutes or until the chicken is well glazed and brown and the marinade is quite thick.

Joint the chicken (see page 10), then, with a heavy cleaver, cut each drumstick and thigh in half. Cut the breasts in half lengthways, then cut each half across into three pieces. Wings are cut into 3 at the joints, and the tips discarded or put into the stock pot. The back may be cut across into 4 pieces, or used for stock if preferred.

In a bowl, combine the shoyu, mirin, sugar, garlic, ginger and sesame oil. Add the chicken pieces and toss to coat, then leave to marinate for at least 1 hour, turning regularly so all the chicken is covered. Drain well, reserving the marinade.

Preheat the oven to 200°C (400°F). Grease a large baking dish and arrange the chicken in a single layer. Roast in the oven for 15 minutes, then turn each piece of chicken over and roast for a further 10 minutes. Reduce the oven temperature to 170°C (340°F). Drain the fat from the baking dish, and spoon some of the marinade over the chicken. Continue cooking for a further 20–25 minutes, basting with the marinade every 10 minutes, until the chicken is tender, well glazed and browned. Serve hot with rice, or cold as an appetiser or picnic food.

Sukiyaki
Quick-cooked beef and vegetables

Serves: 6

1 kg (2 lb 3 oz) scotch fillet in one piece

60 g (2 oz) cellophane (bean thread) noodles or *shirataki* noodles

beef suet or vegetable oil for cooking

12 spring onions (scallions), cut into short lengths

225 g (8 oz) winter bamboo shoots, rinsed, drained and thinly sliced

500 g (1 lb 2 oz) fresh mushrooms, halved or quartered if large

2 onions, cut into eighths

180 g (6½ oz/2 cups) fresh bean sprouts, trimmed

½ small head Chinese cabbage (wombok), chopped

shoyu (Japanese soy sauce) to taste

sugar to taste

sake to taste

beef stock for cooking

6 pieces grilled (broiled) pressed tofu (optional)

6 eggs (optional)

Partially freeze the beef then cut into paper-thin slices. Cook the noodles in a saucepan of boiling water until tender, then drain well and cut into short lengths. Set aside.

Heat the suet or vegetable oil in a large heavy-based frying pan over high heat. Add half the spring onion, bamboo shoot, mushroom, onion, bean sprouts and cabbage to the pan and stir-fry for 1–2 minutes until just tender. Push the vegetables to one side of the pan and add the meat in one layer. When cooked on one side, turn and cook the other side. Sprinkle with shoyu, sugar and sake, to taste, then add a little stock to moisten all the meat and vegetables. Add the noodles and tofu, if using, and heat through. If using shirataki noodles, do not place beside the beef as they are said to toughen the meat.

Serve immediately straight from the pan. Traditionally, each diner breaks an egg into a bowl, beats it lightly with chopsticks, then dips the hot food into it before eating. Cook the remaining vegetables only after the first batch has been eaten. Serve with white rice.

Teppanyaki
Meat and seafood on the griddle

Serves: 4

1 small garlic clove, crushed with
  1 teaspoon sugar

½ teaspoon finely grated fresh ginger

1 tablespoon shoyu (Japanese soy sauce)

500 g (1 lb 2 oz) beef fillet steak, thinly
  sliced

vegetable oil for cooking

1 large green capsicum (bell pepper),
  deseeded and thinly sliced

1 small eggplant (aubergine), cut into
  thin rounds

8 large prawns (shrimp), peeled and
  deveined, tails left intact

12 fresh oysters

Dipping sauce

125 ml (4 fl oz/½ cup) shoyu
  (Japanese soy sauce)

60 ml (2 fl oz/¼ cup) mirin

3 teaspoons sugar

1 teaspoon finely grated fresh ginger

In a bowl, combine the garlic, ginger and shoyu. Add the beef, turning to coat, and leave to marinate for 30 minutes.

To make the dipping sauce, combine the shoyu, mirin, sugar and ginger, stirring to dissolve the sugar. Divide among individual sauce bowls and set aside.

Heat a little vegetable oil on a griddle plate or in a large heavy-based frying pan over medium heat. Cook the capsicum and eggplant – the capsicum first as it requires longer cooking. Add the beef, prawns and oysters as required, cooking only until just done – do not overcook. To serve, dip the ingredients into the sauce and eat with hot white rice.

Gyuniku No Kushiyaki
Beef and spring onions on skewers

Serves: 4–6

500 g (1 lb 2 oz) fillet or rump steak,
    cut into bite-sized cubes

6 spring onions (scallions), cut into
    short lengths

80 ml (2½ fl oz/⅓ cup) shoyu
    (Japanese soy sauce)

2 tablespoons mirin

1 teaspoon sugar

oil for deep-frying

75 g (2¾ oz/½ cup) plain (all-purpose) flour

1 egg, well beaten

165 g (6 oz/1½ cups) dry breadcrumbs

Soak 25 bamboo skewers in water to prevent them from burning during cooking. Thread 3 or 4 pieces of beef and spring onion alternately onto the oiled bamboo skewers.

In a large shallow dish, combine the shoyu, mirin and sugar. Add the skewers, turning to coat, and leave to marinate for at least 30 minutes, or longer if possible. Turn the skewers a few times to make sure all sides are covered.

Heat the oil in a large heavy-based frying pan to 180°C (350°F), or until a cube of bread dropped into the oil turns brown in 15 seconds. Drain the skewers, then dust lightly with flour, shaking off any excess. Dip each skewer into the egg and roll in the breadcrumbs to coat. Gently lower the skewers into the hot oil, a few at a time, and deep-fry until golden brown all over. Drain on paper towel and serve immediately with bowls of hot white rice.

Gyuniku Teriyaki
Grilled marinated beef

Serves: 6

1 small garlic clove, crushed with
  ½ teaspoon sugar

½ teaspoon finely grated fresh ginger

125 ml (4 fl oz/½ cup) shoyu
  (Japanese soy sauce)

125 ml (4 fl oz/½ cup) mirin

6 × 125 g (4½ oz) beef fillet steaks

2 tablespoons oil

2 teaspoons sugar

80 ml (2½ fl oz/⅓ cup) water or Dashi
  (page 32)

1 teaspoon cornflour (cornstarch)

In a bowl, combine the garlic, ginger, shoyu and mirin. Add the steak, turning to coat on both sides, then leave to marinate for about 30 minutes. Drain the steaks, reserving the marinade.

Heat the oil on a griddle plate or in a large heavy-based frying pan over high heat. Cook the steaks for 1 minute, before turning to brown the other side. Reduce the heat and continue cooking until done.

Put the reserved marinade in a small saucepan with the sugar and water and bring to the boil.

In a small bowl, combine the cornflour and 80 ml (2½ fl oz/1/3 cup) cold water and stir to make a smooth paste. Add to the marinade and stir until the sauce boils and becomes clear, then spoon over the steaks. Serve immediately. For easy eating with chopsticks, the steaks should be cut into thin slices and assembled again in their original shape.

Tonkatsu
Pork cutlets

Serves: 4

Ton means pork, and *katsu* is the Japanese pronunciation of 'cutlet'. This is not a traditional dish, but one that has become tremendously popular in recent years. It is said that the Germans introduced this dish to Japan.

80 ml (2½ fl oz/⅓ cup) shoyu
(Japanese soy sauce)

80 ml (2½ fl oz/⅓ cup) mirin

1 garlic clove, crushed

1 pinch of sansho (Japanese pepper) or
black pepper

4 slices pork fillet or bolar blade, cut as
for schnitzel

1 egg, lightly beaten

1 tablespoon finely chopped spring onion
(scallion)

60 g (2 oz/1 cup) panko (Japanese
breadcrumbs) or fresh white breadcrumbs

oil for shallow-frying

pickled ginger (beni shoga) to serve

In a bowl, combine the shoyu, mirin, garlic and sansho. Add the pork and turn to coat both sides, then leave to marinate for 30 minutes.

In a separate bowl, combine the egg and spring onion. Dip the pork first into the egg to coat, and then into the panko, pressing it on firmly. Refrigerate for 1 hour.

Heat the oil in a large heavy-based frying pan over medium heat. Cook the pork until golden brown on both sides. Drain on paper towel. Cut each fillet into slices and assemble again in its original shape. Serve on white rice and garnish with the pickled ginger. A tempura-style dipping sauce may be served separately.

Shabu–Shabu
Simmered steak and vegetables

Serves: 6–8

Shabu-shabu is the Japanese version of Mongolian 'fire pot' or Singapore 'steamboat'. Guests cook their own meal at the table, holding pieces of steak and vegetables with chopsticks and dipping them into boiling stock. The name comes from the gentle swishing sound made as the food is cooked.

1 kg (2 lb 3 oz) beef fillet steak

2 baby carrots, sliced into rounds

1 small head Chinese cabbage (wombok), chopped

12 spring onions (scallions), cut into short lengths

500 g (1 lb 2 oz) button mushrooms, stems removed and halved

2–2.5 litres (68–85 fl oz/8–10 cups) Chicken stock (page 32)

Sesame seed sauce

80 g (2¾ oz/½ cup) toasted, crushed sesame seeds

2 tablespoons rice vinegar or mild white vinegar

190 ml (6½ fl oz/¾ cup) shoyu (Japanese soy sauce)

3 tablespoons finely chopped spring onion (scallion)

2 teaspoons finely grated fresh ginger

Partially freeze the steak, then cut into paper-thin slices and arrange on a serving platter. Cover and refrigerate. Blanch the carrot briefly in a saucepan of boiling water until just tender, refresh under cold running water and drain well. Arrange on a serving platter with the cabbage, spring onion and mushroom, cover and refrigerate. To make the sesame seed sauce combine all the ingredients in a bowl.

When you are ready to serve, put the stock into a shabu-shabu cooker, put the lid on, and fill the chimney with glowing coals. Alternatively, heat an electric frying pan. Keep the stock simmering throughout the meal, adding more as necessary.

The ingredients are picked up with chopsticks and held in the boiling stock until just done, then transferred to individual bowls, dipped in the sauce and eaten with rice. Care should be taken not to overcook the meat and vegetables. Steak should be pale pink when cooked and vegetables tender but still crisp. When all the meat and vegetables are eaten the stock is served as a soup. The bowls should be lifted to the lips, Japanese-style, rather than using a spoon.

Vegetables

❖

Kuya Mushi
Steamed egg custard with tofu

Serves: 4

250 g (9 oz) silken tofu

8 small button mushrooms, sliced

30 g (1 oz/1 cup) watercress sprigs, or
baby English spinach leaves, cut into 5 cm
(2 in) lengths

Custard

4 eggs

625 ml (21 fl oz/2½ cups) Dashi (page 32)
or Chicken stock (page 32)

1½ teaspoons salt

1 tablespoon shoyu (Japanese soy sauce)

2 tablespoons sake or mirin

Drain the tofu on paper towel for 10 minutes. Cut the tofu into 8 equal squares. Put 2 tofu squares each in the base of 4 *chawan mushi* cups or 190 ml (6½ fl oz/¾ cup) capacity ramekins. Divide the mushroom between the cups.

Blanch the watercress or spinach in a saucepan of lightly salted boiling water for 1 minute, then refresh under cold running water and drain well. Pat dry with paper towel, press the watercress into 4 neat portions and set aside.

To make the custard, lightly beat the eggs just until the whites and yolks are mixed. Stir in the dashi, salt, shoyu and sake, then strain the custard and pour over the tofu and mushroom in each ramekin, skimming off any bubbles. Cover the cups with lids or foil.

Put the cups in a saucepan and pour in enough water to come halfway up the sides of the cups. Cover the pan with a folded tea towel (dish towel) and then with the lid. Bring to the boil, then reduce the heat to low and simmer for 10 minutes. After this time, place a portion of the blanched watercress or spinach into each cup, pushing it under the surface of the custard. Replace the covers or foil and continue steaming until the custard is firm. Alternatively, place the cups in a large baking tray and fill the tray with water to come halfway up the sides of the cups. Cook in a 160°C (320°F) oven for 25 minutes. Serve hot.

Nasu Dengaku
Grilled eggplant with miso

Serves: 4

1 eggplant (aubergine), cut into 1.5 cm
    (½ in) rounds or 6 small slender eggplants,
    halved lengthways

2 teaspoons sesame oil

2 tablespoons sweet white miso paste

1 tablespoon sugar

1 tablespoon mirin

1 tablespoon sake or dry sherry

2 tablespoons sesame seeds

Lightly score the surface of the eggplant with the point of a sharp knife and then brush the surface very lightly with sesame oil.

In a bowl, combine all the remaining ingredients, except the sesame seeds, stirring until smooth.

Preheat a grill (broiler) to high and place the eggplant on a tray. Cook the eggplant on each side under the grill, then spoon a scant teaspoon of the miso mixture onto each one. Sprinkle with the sesame seeds and continue cooking until the surface starts to bubble and appears lightly golden. Serve with white rice.

Hijiki Nituke
Seaweed and vegetable sauté

Serves: 4

Before you turn away from the possibility that you may actually like eating seaweed, try this simple vegetarian dish and be prepared for some surprises. The flavour is subtle, the combination pleasing. The fried tofu is optional.

20 g (½ cup) hijiki (dried seaweed), rinsed and drained

2 sheets aburage (deep-fried tofu sheets) (optional)

1 tablespoon vegetable oil

2 teaspoons sesame oil

2 carrots, cut into thin matchsticks

2 onions, thinly sliced

2 tablespoons shoyu (Japanese soy sauce)

80 ml (2½ fl oz/⅓ cup) Dashi (page 32) or water

1 tablespoon sugar

Soak the hijiki in cold water for 30 minutes. Drain well. Put the aburage, if using, in a colander and pour over boiling water to remove some of the oil, then cut into fine strips.

Heat the vegetable and sesame oils in a frying pan over high heat. Add the hijiki, aburage, carrot and onion and stir-fry for 3 minutes. Add the shoyu, dashi and sugar, cover, and simmer for 5 minutes, or until the hijiki and vegetables are tender but not mushy. Serve with white rice.

Sunomono
Vinegared cucumber

Serves: 4

1 telegraph (long) cucumber

1 tablespoon rice vinegar or mild white vinegar

2 teaspoons sugar

½ teaspoon salt

½ teaspoon finely grated fresh ginger

Peel the cucumber, cut in half lengthways, remove the seeds and thinly slice crossways. Combine all the remaining ingredients in a bowl with 1 tablespoon water. Add the cucumber and leave to marinate for at least 1 hour. Serve small helpings as a side salad or relish.

Namasu
Daikon and cabbage salad

Serves: 6

1 large daikon (white radish), peeled and
cut into fine strips

¼ head Chinese cabbage (wombok), finely
shredded

1 carrot, peeled and cut into fine strips

Kimizu dressing (below)

Put the daikon, cabbage and carrot into a bowl of iced water for 1 hour, or until crisp. Drain well and serve with the dressing.

Kimizu
Salad dressing

Makes: about 310 ml (10½ fl oz/1¼ cups)

3 egg yolks

¼ teaspoon salt

1 tablespoon sugar

60 ml (2 fl oz/¼ cup) rice vinegar or
white vinegar

1 tablespoon cornflour (cornstarch)

1 teaspoon prepared wasabi paste or
dry mustard

Put all the ingredients into a food processor with 190 ml (6½ fl oz/¾ cup) water and process until smooth.

Pour the mixture into a small saucepan and cook over low heat, stirring constantly with a wooden spoon, until the mixture thickens and coats the back of the spoon – do not allow it to approach simmering point or it will curdle. Continue stirring after removing from the heat until the dressing is just warm. Refrigerate and use as a salad dressing with sliced raw or crisp-cooked vegetables.

Agedashi Tofu
Tofu in dashi

Serves: 3

....

Dusting the tofu in potato starch gives it the characteristic golden, slightly gummy coating.

....

300 g (10½ oz) silken tofu

375 ml (12½ fl oz/1½ cups) Dashi (page 32)

80 ml (2½ fl oz/⅓ cup) light soy sauce

60 ml (2 fl oz/¼ cup) mirin

3 tablespoons potato starch

oil for deep-frying

3 spring onions (scallions), very thinly sliced

2 teaspoons bonito flakes (katsuobushi)

625 ml (21 fl oz/2½ cups) vegetable oil for frying

1 teaspoon finely grated ginger (optional)

finely grated daikon (white radish) (optional)

Drain the tofu on a few layers of paper towel. Place more layers on top, then place a flat tray on top to help soak up and press out any excess moisture.

Put the dashi into a saucepan with the soy sauce and mirin and bring to the boil. Remove from the heat and set aside.

Cut the tofu in half lengthways, then into thirds to make 6 even-sized squares of tofu. Sift the potato starch onto a plate. Gently turn the tofu in the starch so that there is a light dusting of starch on all sides.

Heat the oil in a frying pan – it should be half the depth of the tofu squares. Place the tofu into the hot oil, turning gently until golden on all sides.

To serve, place 125 ml (4 fl oz/½ cup) of the dashi broth in each bowl and then add 2 cubes of the tofu straight from the frying pan. Sprinkle with the spring onion and bonito flakes and serve immediately. A little grated ginger and daikon may be added to each serve if desired.

Korea

I thought I knew about fine slicing and shredding, having cooked Chinese food for years, but until I was taught how to make some Korean specialities I had no idea just how finely food should be shredded for traditional Korean dishes, such as Guchulpan (page 80). Strips of beef, vegetables and omelette are cut incredibly fine and are uniform in thickness and length.

As part of a guchulpan meal, small pancakes are piled in the centre of a tray (preferably a compartmented tray), surrounded by a selection of ingredients for filling the pancakes, each one shredded finely, stir-fried with a little oil, and seasoned with salt and pepper; where it will not spoil the colour, a little soy sauce is added during cooking. The ingredients are picked up with chopsticks and put in the centre of a pancake, which is rolled around the filling, dipped in a special sauce and eaten.

Guchulpan is usually served as a prelude to a meal or as something to nibble with drinks. I have found it can be a complete dinner – but one of those informal occasions where guests participate more than usual as they become involved in choosing their own fillings, and test their skill at completing the whole operation using chopsticks. Because guchulpan is served at room temperature, it is ideal for advance preparation.

Bean paste is a staple of Korean cooking. The nearest equivalent would be Chinese bean paste or Japanese *aka miso* (fermented soy bean paste), but the Korean version, *dhwen-jang*, has more flavour. According to Koreans it has more nutritional value too. A very salty chilli paste, known as *gochujang*, has a surprisingly mellow flavour, while *silgochu* – thread-fine strips of dried red chilli – are also widely used in Korean cooking.

It is traditional for soy bean pastes and sauces to be made in the spring, and most people make them at home. Equally important is the autumnal pickle-making season when jars of kim chi, the famous Korean pickle based on *baechu* (variously known as Korean cabbage, Chinese cabbage and celery cabbage) are put down in readiness for winter and the year ahead. Daikon (white radish) and cabbage are the favourite vegetables for pickling and large quantities are made, for kim chi appears on the table at every meal, even breakfast.

In Korea, rice is also served at every meal. At breakfast it is sometimes served as gruel, especially for elderly people and children. At other meals steamed rice, cooked by the absorption method, is accompanied by soup, meat, fish, vegetables and, of course, kim chi. Rice is of such importance that meals are described as consisting of rice and *panch'an*, a term that takes in whatever else is served with the rice.

Sometimes the rice is combined with other grains such as barley and beans. Among the beans used are dried cannellini (lima) beans, adzuki beans (small red beans) and soy beans, or soy bean products such as tofu, bean pastes and soy sauce.

Korea has an abundance of fish and other seafood, and often the fish is combined in surprising ways with meat or poultry (see Sin sul lo, page 106). Like the Japanese, Koreans use seaweed, especially the dried seaweed known as *kim* in Korea and *nori* in Japan. It is used as a relish. In order to give it a delicious flavour it should be liberally brushed with sesame oil and sprinkled with salt on one side; the thin sheet is passed back and forth over a hotplate or open flame until it becomes crisp, then it is cut into small squares and served with steamed rice. Rice is wrapped in the seaweed by each diner and rolled up with chopsticks.

Beef is the most popular meat in Korea. Pork and chicken are also used, but mutton (or lamb) never. Beef is not usually cooked in one big piece. It is very thinly sliced and cut into bite-sized pieces; sometimes the slices are beaten out for extra thinness. The beef is then kneaded well with a marinade and left for 2–4 hours to tenderise it and give it flavour.

While Koreans charcoal grill or grill (broil) such meals as *bulgogi* or *bulgalbi*, everyday cooking includes boiling, steaming, stir-frying and deep- or shallow-frying; baking is not one of their cooking methods.

The seven basic flavours of Korean food are garlic, ginger, black pepper, spring onion (scallion), soy sauce, sesame oil and toasted sesame seeds. The sesame seeds are crushed before being added to marinades or mixed with cooked dishes, releasing their full flavour – and it is amazing what a difference the toasting makes to the flavour of sesame. Thus, the Middle Eastern tahini (sesame seed paste), made with untoasted sesame seeds, seems to have no relationship to the sauces of Korea, which are made after the seed has been toasted, giving them a rich nutty flavour.

Korean Marinade

This quantity is sufficient for marinating 500 g (1 lb 2 oz) beef, pork, chicken and most other meats.

½ teaspoon finely grated fresh ginger

1 teaspoon finely chopped garlic

1 teaspoon finely chopped spring onion (scallion)

1 teaspoon sesame oil

1–2 teaspoons toasted, crushed sesame seeds

1 tablespoon light soy sauce

2 teaspoons honey or sugar

¼ teaspoon freshly ground black pepper

Combine all the ingredients in a bowl and stir well until the sugar has dissolved. Add the meat and leave to marinate for 2–4 hours at room temperature before cooking.

Introduction ✦

Serving a Korean meal

Silver chopsticks and spoons are used for Korean meals because silver discolours in the presence of poison, so they are considered the safe way to eat. A formal dinner setting will also have silver bowls for rice and soup. Expensive, but the silverware is usually part of a bride's dowry. Everyday settings are of brass or china. Nowadays stainless steel is more popular than brass because it does not need the polishing that brass does. The spoon is for taking from communal dishes and for serving rice. Soup is also eaten with a spoon, not with lips to the raised bowl, as in Japan.

The food is served and eaten from bowls, not plates. Everything is put on the table at once – hot dishes to the right of the table with the exception of rice which, along with cold dishes, is to the left. The spread of dishes at a typical Korean meal might include rice, soup, fish, chicken, beef, hot sauces, sweet and sour sauces, vegetables prepared in several ways and kim chi of various kinds. There are numerous varieties of kim chi, some prepared with the addition of dried shrimp or salt fish, and elaborate versions including rare fruits and vegetables. Some are very pungent while others are quite mild.

The meal does not generally end with dessert. Sweets are a treat reserved for special occasions such as holidays and festivals. These might take the form of *tteok* – rice cakes filled with sweetened fillings that might include adzuki beans, chestnuts, jujube (a dried red date), sesame seeds, pine nuts and honey. There is also confectionery made from wheat flour, sesame oil and honey, and waffle-like pastries filled with red beans that are made in the shape of a fish (*bungeoppang*) and even a shaved ice dessert, not unlike those found across Southeast Asia, called *patbingsu*. Sometimes fresh fruits are served, or a popular fermented chilled rice and barley flour drink called *sikhae* (pronounced *shikhay*), but this is not the everyday pattern of eating. Korean fruits include apples, Korean pears (like the Japanese nashi pear) oranges, grapes, cherries, plums and persimmons.

Utensils

The traditional Korean kitchen featured wood fires, before the advent of gas and electric stoves. Most of the cooking is quite simple. A good heavy-based frying pan, a wok and some saucepans or flameproof casserole dishes will see you through any of the Korean dishes in this chapter. The only other unusual vessel you need is the traditional pot used in 'steamboat' or 'firekettle' meals if you want to serve *sin sul lo* in true Korean fashion. This pot has a central chimney surrounded by a moat, which holds the broth. It cooks and stays hot at the table because the chimney is filled with glowing coals. Get the coals ready an hour or more beforehand in an outdoor barbecue, a hibachi, a small traditional table-top sized barbecue, or a metal bucket, so they will be well alight and glowing when needed.

The food can be arranged in the pot well ahead of serving time and the whole pot placed in the refrigerator. Just before starting the meal the moat is filled with boiling stock, the cover put on the pot to ensure particles of coal don't fall into the food, and the coals or briquettes (which should be alight and glowing) are transferred to the chimney with tongs. To protect the table, put the pot on a heavy metal tray and put the tray on a thick wooden board. After the broth has simmered for a while, and the contents of the pot are heated through, guests pick out food with chopsticks and eat it with rice and a dipping sauce. At the end of the meal the stock is served as soup.

These pots are often sold at Asian grocery stores. While some models in polished and ornate brass are quite expensive, the modest anodised aluminium versions are inexpensive and work just as well. In Korea, the pots are either individual-sized silver ones, or larger stainless steel versions. Of course you can always substitute an electric frying pan or deep-fryer or wok, three-quarters filled with stock; or use any fairly deep pan on an efficient table burner.

Fresh ingredients

In addition to the items listed opposite, which keep indefinitely, there are the all-important garlic, ginger and spring onions (scallions). Toasted, crushed sesame seed is such an essential item of Korean seasoning that it is useful to prepare a fair amount and store it in readiness for use. To do this, put 155 g (5½ oz/1 cup) white sesame seeds in a heavy-based frying pan and cook over medium heat, stirring constantly, until the sesame seeds are golden brown. As soon as they have acquired the right colour and smell cooked, remove them to a plate or they will darken too much and turn bitter. When slightly cool, crush the seeds using a mortar and pestle or pulverise in a food processor. Cool completely and store in an airtight jar for up to 2 months.

Your Korean shelf

This is a list of spices, sauces and other ingredients which are often used in Korean cooking and that are good to have on hand to make the recipes in this chapter.

bamboo shoots, tinned	peanut oil
black pepper, ground	rice, short-grain
cayenne pepper	rice wine or dry sherry
cellophane (bean thread) noodles	rice vinegar or mild white vinegar
chilli powder	sesame oil
chillies, dried red	sesame seeds
fermented bean sauce (dhwen jang) (see note)	shiitake mushrooms, dried
	soy sauce, light and dark
Korean fermented chilli bean paste (gochujang)	water chestnuts, fresh or tinned
moong dal (split dried mung beans)	

***Note** If fermented bean sauce is unavailable, use Chinese bean paste or Japanese red miso instead.*

Rice, Starters
and Soups

❖

Bokum Bahb
Crab and pork fried rice

Serves: 4

2 tablespoons oil

1 garlic clove, finely grated

1 teaspoon finely grated fresh ginger

85 g (3 oz/½ cup) cooked flaked crabmeat

125 g (4½ oz/½ cup) chopped cooked pork

740 g (1 lb 10 oz/4 cups) hot cooked short-grain rice

6–8 chopped spring onions (scallions)

1 teaspoon salt, or to taste

Heat the oil in a wok or large heavy-based frying pan over medium heat. Add the garlic, ginger, crabmeat and pork and stir-fry until very hot, then add the rice and continue stir-frying until the rice is fried. Add the spring onion and salt to taste, and toss well to combine Serve hot.

Song-I Bahb
Rice with mushrooms

Serves: 6

....

This meal in a pot includes meat, vegetables and rice.

....

1 tablespoon vegetable oil

1 tablespoon sesame oil

2 onions, thinly sliced

100 g (3½ oz/½ cup) finely shredded
   lean steak

250 g (9 oz) fresh button mushrooms, sliced

495 g (1 lb 1 oz/2¼ cups) short-grain rice

1 teaspoon salt

2 tablespoons light soy sauce

¼ teaspoon freshly ground black pepper

2 tablespoons toasted, crushed sesame seeds

Heat the vegetable and sesame oils in a large saucepan over medium heat. Add the onion, steak and mushroom and stir-fry for 2 minutes, then add the rice and stir-fry for a further 1 minute. Add all the remaining ingredients and 750 ml (25½ fl oz/3 cups) hot water and bring to the boil, then reduce the heat to low, cover, and cook for 20 minutes – do not lift the lid or stir during this time. Serve hot with pickles or vegetable dishes.

Guchulpan
Nine varieties

Serves: 12 as an appetiser, 6 as a main dish

Guchulpan is usually served as a prelude to a meal or to accompany drinks. Small pancakes are piled in the centre of a tray, around which are a selection of finely shredded omelettes, stir-fried shredded beef and various vegetables for filling them. The ingredients are picked up with chopsticks and put in the centre of a pancake, which is rolled around the filling, dipped in a special sauce and eaten. Served at room temperature, it is ideal for making in advance.

Pancakes

225 g (8 oz/1½ cups) plain (all-purpose) flour

¼ teaspoon salt

2 eggs, lightly beaten

250 ml (8½ fl oz/1 cup) milk

vegetable oil for frying

pine nuts and parsley sprigs (optional) to garnish

Fillings

10 dried shiitake mushrooms

vegetable oil or sesame oil for frying

soy sauce to taste

sugar for sprinkling

3 eggs, separated

250 g (9 oz) beef fillet

3 carrots, cut into thin strips

12 spring onions (scallions), cut into thin strips

1 large daikon (white radish), peeled and cut into thin strips

250 g (9 oz) zucchini (courgettes), cut into thin strips

Dipping sauce

190 ml (6½ fl oz/¾ cup) soy sauce

1 tablespoon mild vinegar

1 tablespoon toasted, crushed sesame seeds

2 tablespoons finely chopped spring onion (scallion)

To make the pancakes, sift the flour and salt into a bowl and make a well in the centre. In a separate bowl, mix together the egg, milk and 250 ml (8½ fl oz/1 cup) water. Add to the flour and stir rapidly with a wooden spoon to combine, beating until smooth. Set aside while preparing the fillings.

To make the fillings, soak the mushrooms in hot water for 20–30 minutes. Drain, reserving 125 ml (4 fl oz/½ cup) of the soaking liquid, then cut off and discard the stems and thinly slice the caps.

Heat a little oil in a wok or large heavy-based frying pan over high heat. Add the mushroom, soy sauce, freshly ground black pepper, the reserved soaking liquid and a sprinkling of sugar. Cover the pan and simmer for 15–20 minutes, or until the mushroom is tender and all the liquid has been absorbed. Set aside.

Beat the egg yolks and egg whites in separate bowls. Heat a little oil in the clean wok and separately fry the yolks and whites to make large, flat omelettes – do not allow to brown. Allow to cool, then slice into very fine strips.

Partially freeze the beef then slice it very thinly. Continue to slice into shreds. Heat a little oil in the clean wok over high heat and stir-fry the beef, adding soy sauce and pepper, to taste – the beef should be well done and any liquid absorbed.

In separate batches, add a little oil to the wok and stir-fry the carrot, spring onion, daikon and zucchini, seasoning with salt and pepper to taste. The aim is to keep the natural colour of the vegetables so cook for only a short time and do not allow anything to brown. Arrange all the filling ingredients in separate piles around the edge of a plate or in a compartmented tray, leaving the centre for the pancakes. Set aside.

To cook the pancakes, heat a little vegetable oil in a wok or large heavy-based frying pan over medium–low heat. Pour in a ladleful of the batter, sufficient to make a fairly thin pancake and cook until set. Turn and cook the other side, then remove to a large chopping board. When all the pancakes have been made, use a round pastry cutter with a 7.5 cm (3 in) diameter to make small circles. Pile the pancakes into the centre of the tray or dish and garnish with a few pine nuts and parsley sprigs, if desired.

To make the dipping sauce, combine all the ingredients and divide between individual sauce bowls to serve.

Ganghwe
Appetisers

Makes: about 15

375 g (13 oz) beef fillet

Korean marinade (page 73)

2 eggs, separated

sesame oil for frying

spring onions (scallions), green part only,
  or chives to serve

dried red chilli, thinly sliced

Slice the beef into very fine shreds and marinate in a bowl with the Korean marinade for 20 minutes.

Beat the egg yolks and egg whites in separate bowls. Heat a little sesame oil in a wok or large heavy-based frying pan over low heat. Add the egg yolk and swirl to make a paper-thin omelette; when set, turn and lightly cook the other side. Remove to a plate. Repeat with the egg white to make another omelette. Cut the omelettes into thin strips and set aside.

Stir-fry the beef in a dry wok or large heavy-based frying pan for 3 minutes, or until brown. Set aside.

Pour boiling water over the spring onions to make them pliable. Drain well and cool slightly.

To serve, make little bundles of egg strips, beef strips and strips of dried chilli and tie them together with the spring onion, leaving strips of egg and beef showing at either end. Serve with Sesame seed sauce (below).

Cho Kanjang
Sesame seed sauce

Makes: 250 ml (8½ fl oz/1 cup)

80 g (2¾ oz/½ cup) toasted, crushed sesame
  seeds

1 tablespoon sugar

60 ml (2 fl oz/¼ cup) vinegar

80 ml (2½ fl oz/⅓ cup) light soy sauce

Put all the ingredients into a bowl and stir well to combine. Serve with hot or cold vegetables or as a sauce for meat. This sauce can be stored in an airtight container in the refrigerator for up to 2 weeks.

Bindaettoek

Bean pancakes

Makes: about 20

220 g (8 oz/1 cup) moong dal (split dried
  mung beans)

2 eggs, lightly beaten

125 g (4½ oz) minced (ground) pork

1 small onion, finely chopped

1 spring onion (scallion), thinly sliced

2 garlic cloves, crushed

1 teaspoon salt

¼ teaspoon freshly ground black pepper

1 teaspoon finely grated fresh ginger

45 g (1½ oz/½ cup) fresh bean sprouts,
  trimmed and chopped

40 g (1½ oz/½ cup) Kim chi (page 114) or
  shredded Chinese cabbage (wombok)

2 tablespoons sesame oil, plus extra for
  cooking

Wash the moong dal and soak in cold water overnight. Rinse
and drain well.

Put the moong dal and 250 ml (8½ fl oz/1 cup) water into a
food processor and process until smooth. Transfer to a bowl,
add all the remaining ingredients, except the extra sesame
oil and mix well.

Heat a little sesame oil on a griddle plate or in a large heavy-
based frying pan over medium heat. Drop 1 tablespoonful
of the mixture into the pan at a time and cook until golden
brown underneath, then turn and cook the other side. Serve
hot or cold.

Yook Soo
Beef stock

Makes: 3 litres (101 fl oz/12 cups)

2 kg (4 lb 6 oz) beef rib bones

1 kg (2 lb 3 oz) beef shin (shank)

4 large slices fresh ginger

1 teaspoon salt

Put the well-washed bones into a large saucepan with the beef, ginger, salt and enough cold water to cover. Bring to the boil. Remove any scum that rises to the surface, then reduce the heat to low, cover, and simmer for 2–3 hours. Remove from the heat, allow to cool then strain the stock and chill. Remove any trace of fat from the surface before using. Use as basic stock in soups.

Gorigomtang
Oxtail soup

Serves: 6–8

1.5 kg (3 lb 5 oz) oxtail, jointed

2 slices fresh ginger

1 teaspoon salt

Sauce

60 ml (2 fl oz/¼ cup) light soy sauce

1 tablespoon sesame oil

1 tablespoon toasted, crushed sesame seeds

¼ teaspoon freshly ground black pepper

3 tablespoons finely chopped spring onions (scallions)

3 teaspoons finely chopped garlic

1 teaspoon finely chopped ginger

Put the oxtail into a large saucepan with the ginger, salt and 2 litres (68 fl oz/8 cups) water. Bring to the boil, then reduce the heat to low and simmer for about 2 hours, or until the meat is tender – you should have about 1.5 litres (51 fl oz/6 cups) stock. Remove any scum that rises to the surface.

In a bowl, combine the sauce ingredients and serve with the soup as a dipping sauce for the pieces of oxtail.

Gogi Kuk
Beef and vegetable soup

Serves: 4–6

Like many Korean dishes, this soup has a hot tang from the bean sauce.

4 dried shiitake mushrooms

2 tablespoons oil

250 g (9 oz) round steak, diced

3 spring onions (scallions), cut into 5 cm (2 in) lengths

2 garlic cloves, finely chopped

1.5 litres (51 fl oz/6 cups) Beef stock (opposite) or water

1 teaspoon Korean fermented chilli bean paste (gochujang), or to taste (glossary)

2 tablespoons light soy sauce

1½ teaspoons salt

1 tablespoon rice wine or dry sherry

½ teaspoon freshly ground black pepper

1 teaspoon sesame oil

Soak the mushrooms in hot water for 20–30 minutes. Drain, then cut off and discard the stems and thinly slice the caps. Set aside.

Heat the oil in a large saucepan over medium heat. Add the beef and stir-fry until browned. Add the spring onion, garlic and mushroom and stir-fry for a further 1 minute, then add all the remaining ingredients except the sesame oil. Bring to the boil, stir well, then reduce the heat to low and simmer for 10 minutes. Taste and season as necessary. Add the sesame oil, stir to combine and serve immediately.

Mandoo
Dumpling soup

Serves: 6

2.25 litres (76 fl oz/9 cups) Beef stock (page 84)

2 tablespoons light soy sauce

omelette strips to garnish

toasted nori sheets, crumbled, to garnish

Dumplings

2 tablespoons oil

125 g (4½ oz) minced (ground) pork

125 g (4½ oz) lean minced (ground) beef

180 g (6½ oz/2 cups) fresh bean sprouts, trimmed

½ head small Chinese cabbage (wombok)

90 g (3 oz) silken tofu

3 spring onions (scallions), thinly sliced

1 tablespoon toasted, crushed sesame seeds

1 garlic clove, finely chopped

½ teaspoon salt

¼ teaspoon freshly ground black pepper

150 g (5½ oz) won ton wrappers

To make the dumplings, heat the oil in a saucepan over medium heat. Add the pork and beef minces and cook until the meat changes colour. Add 125 ml (4 fl oz/½ cup) water and simmer gently until the liquid evaporates. Set aside.

Blanch the bean sprouts in lightly salted boiling water for 3 minutes, then remove with a slotted spoon and chop. Boil the cabbage for 5 minutes, drain well and finely chop. Mash the tofu. Mix all these ingredients with the spring onion, sesame seeds and garlic, salt and pepper.

Place a teaspoonful of the filling in the centre of each won ton wrapper, dampen the edges with water and fold over and press together to form a triangle. Cover with plastic wrap so they don't dry out – they may be made up to 3 hours in advance and refrigerated.

Put the stock, soy sauce and some salt in a large saucepan and bring to the boil. Gently lower the dumplings into the stock, taking care they do not stick together, and simmer, in batches, for 10 minutes, or until they rise to the surface and are cooked. Serve immediately in small bowls with the omelette strips and crumbled nori to garnish.

Kong Namul Kuk
Soup of soy bean sprouts

Serves: 6

1 tablespoon soy sauce

1 tablespoon sesame oil

¼ teaspoon freshly ground black pepper

2 garlic cloves, crushed

375 g (13 oz) lean steak, thinly sliced

390 g (14 oz/4⅓ cups) fresh soy bean
sprouts, trimmed

2 spring onions (scallions), green part only,
thinly sliced

Put the soy sauce, sesame oil, pepper and garlic in a bowl.
Add the beef and toss to coat in the marinade.

Heat a wok over high heat and stir-fry the beef until it
changes colour. Add 2 litres (68 fl oz/8 cups) water and
the bean sprouts, bring to the boil, then reduce the heat
to low, cover, and simmer for 30 minutes. Remove from
the heat, add the spring onion, re-cover and simmer for a
further 5 minutes. Add more soy sauce or some salt if desired
and serve hot.

Seafood

❖

Saewoo Bokum
Green beans with prawns

Serves: 6

....

500 g (1 lb 2 oz) small raw prawns (shrimp),
  peeled and deveined

500 g (1 lb 2 oz) fresh green beans, trimmed

2 tablespoons vegetable oil

1 tablespoon sesame oil

1 onion, thinly sliced

60 ml (2 fl oz/¼ cup) light soy sauce

1 teaspoon sugar

3 teaspoons toasted, crushed sesame seeds

Roughly chop the prawns and set aside. Cut the beans into thin diagonal slices.

Heat the vegetable and sesame oils in a wok or large heavy-based frying pan over high heat. Add the onion and the prawn meat and stir-fry for 2 minutes, then add the beans and stir-fry for a further 3 minutes. Add the soy sauce, sugar and sesame seeds and toss to combine, then cover and simmer over low heat for 6–8 minutes, or until the beans are just tender – they must not be overcooked. Serve immediately with rice.

Tuigim Saengsun
Fried fish

Serves: 6

6 small boneless, skinless, firm, white fish fillets

2 tablespoons light soy sauce

2 tablespoons toasted, crushed sesame seeds

a pinch of freshly ground black pepper

2 tablespoons finely chopped spring onion (scallion)

2 teaspoons sesame oil

2 tablespoons vegetable oil

Wipe the fish with damp paper towel. In a bowl, combine the soy sauce, sesame seeds, pepper, spring onion and sesame oil. Add the fish and turn to coat in the marinade.

Heat the vegetable oil in a wok or large heavy-based frying pan and cook the fish until golden brown on both sides. Serve the fried fish while it is warm.

Gun Saengsun
Grilled fish

Serves: 6

6 small whole fish or 12 small firm white fish fillets

60 ml (2 fl oz/¼ cup) soy sauce

2 teaspoons sugar

1 tablespoon toasted, crushed sesame seeds

1 tablespoon sesame oil

1 garlic clove, crushed

1 teaspoon finely grated fresh ginger

½ teaspoon chilli sauce (optional)

Clean and scale the fish, leaving the head on. Wipe inside the fish cavity with damp paper towel that has first been dipped in coarse salt. Trim any long spines or fins neatly.

In a bowl, combine all the remaining ingredients. Pour over the fish, turning to coat.

Place the fish on an oiled grill (broiler) tray and grill under medium heat until the fish is cooked through to the centre bone. Better still, grill over glowing coals. Brush the fish with the sauce during cooking to keep the flesh moist. Do not overcook.

Seafood ❖

Meat

❖

Dak Busutjim
Braised chicken and mushrooms

Serves: 4–6

10 dried shiitake mushrooms

1 kg (2 lb 3 oz) whole chicken

60 ml (2 fl oz/¼ cup) light soy sauce

1 tablespoon sesame oil

2 garlic cloves, crushed

½ teaspoon cayenne pepper or chilli powder

½ teaspoon freshly ground black pepper

2 tablespoons vegetable oil

1 large onion, cut into large pieces

2 tinned winter bamboo shoots, cut into
thin matchsticks

4 spring onions (scallions), cut into short
lengths

2 tablespoons toasted, crushed sesame
seeds to garnish

Soak the mushrooms in hot water for 20–30 minutes. Drain, reserving 125 ml (4 fl oz/½ cup) of the soaking liquid, then cut off and discard the stems and thinly slice the caps. Set aside.

Joint the chicken (see page 10), then chop into small pieces, cutting through the bones with a heavy cleaver.

In a bowl, mix together the soy sauce, sesame oil, garlic, cayenne pepper and black pepper and rub over the chicken to coat. Leave to marinate for 30 minutes. Drain well, reserving the marinade.

Heat the vegetable oil in a wok or large heavy-based frying pan over medium heat. Add the chicken and stir-fry until brown. Add the mushroom, reserved soaking liquid and the reserved marinade, cover, and simmer for 15–20 minutes, or until the chicken is tender. Add the onion, bamboo shoot and spring onion and cook for a further 2 minutes. Garnish with the sesame seeds and serve with white rice.

Dak Jim
Chicken stew

Serves: 4–6

1.5 kg (3 lb 5 oz) whole chicken

60 ml (2 fl oz/¼ cup) light soy sauce

2 tablespoons sesame oil

1 tablespoon finely chopped garlic

½ teaspoon chilli powder or cayenne pepper

3 spring onions (scallions), finely chopped

¼ teaspoon salt

Joint the chicken (see page 10) and cut into serving pieces.

Put the chicken into a large heavy-based saucepan with all the remaining ingredients and toss to coat the chicken. Leave for 2 hours at room temperature.

Place the pan over low heat, cover, and cook the chicken for about 2 hours, or until the chicken is cooked through. Serve with hot rice and Kim chi (page 114).

Yukkae Jang Kuk
Beef stew

Serves: 6

---

1 kg (2 lb 3 oz) skirt (flank) steak

2 teaspoons salt

½ teaspoon freshly ground black pepper

125 g (4½ oz) rice vermicelli (rice-stick) noodles

24 spring onions (scallions), thinly sliced

1 teaspoon sugar

2 tablespoons sesame oil

2 teaspoons chilli powder, or to taste

2 eggs, lightly beaten

Put the whole steak into a large saucepan with the salt, pepper and just enough water to cover. Bring to the boil, then reduce the heat to low, cover, and simmer for 1½ hours, or until the steak is very tender. Remove from the heat and allow to cool, then use your fingers to shred the meat into small pieces.

Soak the rice vermicelli according to the packet instructions, then drain well.

Return the meat to the pan, add the spring onion and sugar and simmer over low heat for 10 minutes. Add the rice vermicelli with the combined sesame oil and chilli powder – the rich red oil will float to the top. Dribble the egg into the simmering stew, stirring so that it cooks in shreds. Serve with hot white rice.

Gogi Bokum
Deep-fried beef slices

Serves: 3–4

500 g (1 lb 2 oz) lean rump or fillet steak

1 spring onion (scallion), finely chopped

1 tablespoon finely chopped leek, white part only

1 garlic clove, finely chopped

½ teaspoon sugar

1 tablespoon light soy sauce

2 teaspoons sesame oil

a few drops of hot chilli sauce or chilli oil

125 ml (4 fl oz/½ cup) peanut oil

1 quantity Bulgogi sauce (page 100)

Cut the steak into very thin slices and beat them quite flat. Arrange in a single layer in a large dish and sprinkle over the spring onion, leek and garlic.

In a bowl, combine the sugar, soy sauce, sesame oil and chilli sauce. Spoon over the beef and leave to marinate for 2–3 hours, or longer in the refrigerator.

Heat the peanut oil in a wok or large heavy-based frying pan over high heat. Add the beef slices, a few at a time, for a few seconds until they change colour. Remove from the heat and drain briefly, then serve at once. To serve, the steak is dipped in the bulgogi sauce and eaten accompanied by steamed white rice.

Bulgalbi
Barbecued short ribs of beef

Serves: 8–10 as an appetiser, 4 as a main dish

2 kg (4 lb 6 oz) beef short ribs, cut into 5 cm
(2 in) lengths (ask your butcher to do this)

Bulgalbi marinade

125 ml (4 fl oz/½ cup) soy sauce

4 tablespoons finely chopped spring onion
(scallion)

2 teaspoons crushed garlic

1 teaspoon finely grated fresh ginger

1 tablespoon sugar

½ teaspoon freshly ground black pepper

2 tablespoons toasted, crushed sesame seeds

To make the bulgalbi marinade, combine all the ingredients
in a large bowl with 125 ml (4 fl oz/½ cup) water.

Put the ribs on a chopping board, bone side down, and use
a sharp knife to cut halfway through the meat in small
dice – this will allow the marinade to penetrate. Add to the
marinade and turn to coat, then cover and leave to marinate
for at least 4 hours, or refrigerate overnight.

Prepare a domed grill or table-top barbecue well ahead of
cooking time so the coals have an hour or more to achieve
the steady glow necessary for successful cooking. Put the
meat on the grill, bone side down, and cook until brown.
Turn and cook the other side until well done. Turn the beef
frequently, so that all sides are brown and crisp. The short
ribs are intended to be picked up with the fingers for eating.

Note

*Bulgalbi can also be cooked under a
preheated grill (broiler) or oven-roasted.
Short ribs should be cooked in one layer in
a roasting tin. Roast in a 200°C (400°F)
oven for 1 hour, turning the beef halfway
through cooking.*

Bulgogi
Fiery beef

Serves: 10–12 as an appetiser, 6–8 as a main dish

....

1 kg (2 lb 3 oz) lean rump or fillet

½ quantity Bulgalbi marinade (page 99)

1 quantity Bulgogi sauce (below)

Cut the steak into very thin slices. Beat them out very flat, then cut into medium-sized squares. Place in a dish with the marinade, turning to coat and leave the meat to marinate for 3 hours or longer in the refrigerator. Grill briefly over glowing coals or in a chargrill pan and serve with rice and the bulgogi sauce.

Yangnyum Kanjang
Bulgogi sauce

Makes: 125 ml (4 fl oz/½ cup)

....

60 ml (2 fl oz/1/4 cup) soy sauce

2 teaspoons sesame oil

1 teaspoon fermented bean sauce (dhwen jang) or Chinese bean paste

2 tablespoons rice wine or dry sherry

1 teaspoon toasted, crushed sesame seeds

2 teaspoons finely chopped spring onion (scallion)

½–1 teaspoon Korean fermented chilli bean paste (gochujang) or chilli sauce (optional)

1 small garlic clove, crushed

salt to taste

2 teaspoons sugar

In a small bowl, combine the soy sauce, sesame oil, fermented bean sauce, 2 tablespoons water, rice wine, sesame seeds, spring onion and fermented chilli bean paste, if using.

Crush together the garlic, salt and sugar to a fine paste. Add to the soy mixture and stir well to combine. Serve in small individual sauce dishes or use as directed.

Yang Pa Wa Sogogi Jjim
Braised beef with onions

Serves: 4–6

6 dried shiitake mushrooms

750 g (1 lb 11 oz) lean round or topside steak

3 tablespoons toasted, crushed sesame seeds

1 garlic clove

½ teaspoon finely chopped fresh ginger

60 ml (2 fl oz/¼ cup) light soy sauce

½ teaspoon chilli powder or cayenne pepper

2 tablespoons vegetable oil

24 spring onions (scallions), white part only, thinly sliced

Soak the mushrooms in hot water for 20–30 minutes. Drain, then cut off and discard the stems and thinly slice the caps. Set aside.

Slice the beef and cut into bite-sized squares, then beat until very thin.

In a bowl, combine the sesame seeds, garlic, ginger, soy sauce and chilli powder. Add the beef and use your hands to knead the seasonings into the meat.

Heat the vegetable oil in a wok or large heavy-based frying pan over high heat. Add the beef and mushroom and stir-fry until cooked. Remove to a plate, then add the spring onion to the wok and stir-fry, adding a little more oil if necessary. Scatter the spring onion over the meat and serve immediately – this dish should be eaten with bowls of hot rice.

Gogi Busut Bokum
Stir-fried beef with fresh mushrooms

Serves: 2–4

250 g (9 oz) lean steak

1 small garlic clove, crushed

½ teaspoon finely grated fresh ginger

½ teaspoon salt

2 tablespoons oil

250 g (9 oz) fresh button, field or fresh shiitake mushrooms, thickly sliced

60 ml (2 fl oz/¼ cup) beef stock or hot water

1½ teaspoons cornflour (cornstarch)

Partially freeze the beef, then cut into paper-thin slices.

In a bowl, mix together the garlic, ginger and salt. Add the beef and toss to coat the meat evenly.

Heat the oil in a wok or large heavy-based frying pan over high heat. Add the beef and stir-fry until the meat changes colour. Add the mushroom and stir-fry for a further minute, then add the stock, reduce the heat to low, cover, and simmer for 2 minutes.

In a small bowl, combine the cornflour and 1 tablespoon cold water to make a smooth paste. Push the beef and mushrooms to one side of the wok, stir in the cornflour paste and stir constantly until the sauce boils and thickens. Serve immediately with white rice.

Meat

Dweji Galbi Wa Cham Gi Leum
Spareribs braised with sesame sauce

Serves: 4–5

1 tablespoon oil

1.5 kg (3 lb 5 oz) pork spareribs, cut into 5 cm (2 in) lengths (ask your butcher to do this)

2 tablespoons soy sauce

2 teaspoons sesame oil

3 spring onions (scallions), thinly sliced, plus extra to garnish

2 garlic cloves, crushed

1 teaspoon finely grated fresh ginger

2 tablespoons sugar

2 tablespoons rice wine or dry sherry

1 tablespoon toasted, crushed sesame seeds

1 teaspoon cornflour (cornstarch)

Heat the oil in a wok or large heavy-based frying pan over high heat. Add the spareribs and cook to brown all over.

In a bowl, combine the soy sauce, sesame oil, spring onion, garlic, ginger, sugar, rice wine, sesame seeds and 250 ml (8½ fl oz/1 cup) hot water. Add to the wok, bring to the boil, then reduce the heat to low, cover, and simmer for 40–45 minutes.

In a small bowl, combine the cornflour and 1 tablespoon cold water and stir to make a smooth paste. Add to the wok and stir constantly over medium heat until the sauce boils and thickens. Serve hot, garnished with the extra spring onion. Serve with white rice.

Sanjuck
Skewered beef and mushrooms

Serves: 4–5

250 g (9 oz) lean rump or round steak

2 tablespoons sesame oil

1 tablespoon soy sauce

2 teaspoons toasted, crushed sesame seeds

1 garlic clove, crushed with ½ teaspoon sugar

1 pinch of freshly ground black pepper

½ teaspoon crushed fresh chilli

12 spring onions (scallions), cut into 5 cm (2 in) lengths

185 g (6½ oz) button mushrooms, thickly sliced

oil for frying

plain (all-purpose) flour for dipping

2 large eggs, lightly beaten

Soak 25 bamboo skewers in water to prevent them from burning during cooking. Cut the beef into 5 mm (¼ in) strips, then cut each strip into 5 cm (2 in) lengths.

In a bowl, combine the sesame oil, soy sauce, sesame seeds, garlic, pepper and chilli. Add the beef, toss to coat, then leave to marinate while preparing the other ingredients.

Thread the meat, spring onion and mushrooms alternately onto each skewer. Cut the skewers in half if they are too long to fit into your frying pan, but thread two lots of ingredients on before you cut them so you have the pointed end for easy threading.

Heat enough oil to cover the base of a large heavy-based frying pan – the oil should be hot, but not smoking. Dip the skewers first into the flour, then into the egg. Cook the skewers until brown and crisp, about 2–3 minutes on each side. Serve immediately with white rice.

Sin Sul Lo
Banquet firepot

Serves: 6

In Korea, this version of the famous steamboat is served on special occasions. All the food is arranged in the pot before it is brought to the table to finish cooking. It is also sometimes served in individual pots with coals in the central chimney to keep the broth simmering throughout the meal.

500 g (1 lb 2 oz) fillet steak

2 onions, sliced

250 g (9 oz) boneless, skinless, firm, white fish fillets, sliced

250 g (9 oz) calves' livers, sliced

3 eggs, separated

plain (all-purpose) flour

vegetable oil for frying

4 spring onions (scallions)

1 carrot

60 g (2 oz/½ cup) walnuts

80 g (2¾ oz/½ cup) pine nuts

1.5–2 litres (49–68 fl oz/6–8 cups) Beef stock (page 84), boiling

Sesame seed sauce (page 82)

Partially freeze the beef, then cut into paper-thin slices. Put the beef and onions into a *sin sul lo* pot (steamboat) or individual pots.

Season the fish and liver with salt and freshly ground black pepper. Beat the yolk of 1 egg and dip slices of liver in it, then turn to coat in the flour. Lightly beat 1 egg white and dip the fish slices in it, then turn to coat in the flour.

Heat just enough vegetable oil to cover the base of a frying pan over high heat. Quickly sauté the fish and liver separately until just cooked. Put these in the pot on top of the beef and onion.

Separately beat the remaining egg yolk and egg whites and cook in a frying pan to make 2 separate omelettes. Cut each omelette into strips just long enough to fit across the moat of the firepot. Cut the spring onions into similar lengths. Slice the carrot thinly and cut into strips of the same size. Arrange these over the beef, fish and liver, then garnish with the walnuts and pine nuts. The recipe may be prepared up to this point, covered and refrigerated until ready to serve.

At serving time, carefully ladle the boiling stock into the moat without disturbing the arrangement of food. Replace the cover on the pot and use tongs to place the glowing coals into the chimney. Bring to the table and allow the broth to simmer for a few minutes and heat the contents of the pot thoroughly.

Remove the cover and let guests help themselves from the pot with chopsticks. They dip the food in individual bowls of sesame seed sauce before eating. Boiled rice is served with this meal and at the end the stock is served as soup.

Oyi Jikai
Stir-fried cucumbers with beef

Serves: 4

....

250 g (9 oz) lean rump or fillet steak

2 teaspoons sesame oil

1 tablespoon light soy sauce

½ teaspoon salt

½ teaspoon sugar

¼ teaspoon cayenne pepper

2 telegraph (long) cucumbers

1 tablespoon vegetable oil

2 tablespoons toasted, crushed sesame seeds

Partially freeze the beef, then cut into paper-thin slices.

In a bowl, combine the sesame oil, soy sauce, salt, sugar and cayenne pepper. Add the beef and mix well by hand so the flavourings penetrate the meat.

Peel the cucumbers, leaving a thin strip of green skin at intervals for decorative effect. Cut each in half lengthways, scoop out the seeds then cut widthways into thin slices.

Heat the vegetable oil in a wok or large heavy-based frying pan over high heat. Add the beef and stir-fry for 1 minute. Add the cucumber and stir-fry for a further 1 minute, then let the mixture simmer until the cucumber is tender but still crisp. Garnish with the sesame seeds and serve hot with white rice.

Chap Chye
Stir-fried mixture

Serves: 4–6

250 g (9 oz) beef fillet

1 teaspoon sugar

1 tablespoon soy sauce

2 teaspoons finely chopped spring onion (scallion)

1 teaspoon finely chopped garlic

1 teaspoon toasted, crushed sesame seeds

¼ teaspoon freshly ground black pepper

1 tablespoon sesame oil

60 g (2 oz) cellophane (bean thread) noodles

2 eggs, separated

vegetable oil for frying

125 g (4½ oz/1⅔ cups) thinly sliced Chinese cabbage (wombok) (optional)

205 g (7 oz/1⅓ cups) thinly sliced carrots

185 g (6½ oz/¾ cup) thinly sliced bamboo shoots

125 g (4½ oz) onions, thinly sliced

2 cucumbers, thinly sliced

200 g (7 oz) English spinach, trimmed and sliced

sugar to taste

soy sauce to taste

Partially freeze the beef, then cut into paper-thin slices.

In a bowl combine the sugar, soy sauce, spring onion, garlic, sesame seeds, pepper and sesame oil. Add the beef and toss to coat, then leave to marinate for 30 minutes.

Soak the noodles in hot water for 20 minutes, then drain well and cut into 8 cm (3¼ in) lengths.

Separately beat the egg yolks and egg whites and cook in a frying pan to make 2 separate omelettes. Cut each omelette into strips. Set aside.

Heat a little vegetable oil in a wok or large heavy-based frying pan and separately stir-fry the beef, noodles, cabbage, if using, carrot, bamboo shoots, onion, cucumber and spinach until just cooked.

To serve, mix all the ingredients together on a large plate, season to taste with the soy sauce, sugar, salt and freshly ground black pepper. Serve very hot.

Sikumchi Kuk
Braised spinach with pork

Serves: 6

2 tablespoons oil

250 g (9 oz) pork fillet, diced

2 garlic cloves, finely chopped

400 g (14 oz) fresh English spinach,
    trimmed and chopped into large pieces

2 tablespoons light soy sauce

¼ teaspoon freshly ground black pepper

5 spring onions (scallions), thinly sliced

1 egg, lightly beaten

3 tablespoons toasted, crushed sesame seeds

Heat the oil in a wok or large heavy-based frying pan over high heat. Add the pork and garlic and stir-fry until the meat changes colour. Add the spinach and toss well, season with the soy sauce and pepper, reduce the heat to low, cover, and simmer until the spinach is tender. Add the spring onion and egg and stir-fry over medium heat for 2 minutes, then sprinkle with the sesame seeds and serve hot with rice.

Song-I Busut Jim
Steamed mushrooms with prawn and chicken

Serves: 4

250 g (9 oz) button mushrooms (choose mushrooms of equal size, with about 3.5 cm/1½ in diameters)

125 g (4½ oz) raw prawns (shrimp), peeled, deveined and finely chopped

1 boneless skinless chicken breast, finely chopped

6 water chestnuts, chopped

2 tablespoons chopped bamboo shoot

2 tablespoons finely chopped spring onion (scallion)

1 tablespoon cornflour (cornstarch)

1 tablespoon light soy sauce

1 teaspoon oyster sauce

½ teaspoon salt

½ teaspoon finely grated fresh ginger

fresh coriander (cilantro) leaves to garnish (optional)

Remove the mushroom stems with a little twist, leaving the caps intact. (Reserve the stems for another use.)

In a bowl, combine all the other ingredients, mixing thoroughly. Fill each mushroom cap with this mixture, creating a little mound and pressing into a neat shape. Put the mushrooms on a lightly oiled heatproof plate and steam for 20 minutes. Garnish with the coriander, if using, and serve at room temperature.

Vegetables

❖

Mu Saingchai
Daikon salad

Serves: 4

1–2 crisp cooking apples, peeled and cut into thin matchsticks

juice of ½ lemon

2 large daikon (white radishes), peeled and cut into thin matchsticks

3 spring onions (scallions), thinly sliced

Dressing

3 tablespoons light soy sauce

1 tablespoon light olive oil

2 teaspoons sesame oil

60 ml (2 fl oz/¼ cup) rice vinegar or mild white vinegar

3 teaspoons sugar

1 teaspoon salt

1 tablespoon toasted, crushed sesame seeds

1 fresh red chilli, deseeded and finely chopped

To make the dressing, combine all the ingredients in a small bowl.

Soak the apple in cold water with a good squeeze of lemon juice to prevent discoloration. Drain well.

Combine the daikon, apple and spring onion in a serving bowl with the dressing and toss to combine. Cover and refrigerate before serving.

Vegetables

Kim Chi
Pickled Chinese cabbage

Makes: 750 g

Kim chi is one of Korea's national dishes, with as many versions as there are cooks. This is a combination of three recipes, and while it may have an unorthodox touch in the Japanese dashi stock, it is a very tasty version of kim chi.

1 large head Chinese cabbage (wombok)

salt (not iodised)

cayenne pepper

6 spring onions (scallions), thinly sliced

6 garlic cloves, finely chopped

3 fresh red chillies, deseeded and finely chopped

1 teaspoon finely chopped fresh ginger

500 ml (17 fl oz/2 cups) Dashi (page 32)

2 teaspoons light soy sauce

Cut the base off the cabbage, then slice lengthways into 6 segments. Dry in the sun for half a day, cut each segment in half widthways, then put into an unglazed earthenware pot alternately with good handfuls of salt and a sprinkling of cayenne pepper, making several layers. Cover with a wooden lid just small enough to fit inside the pot so that it rests directly on the cabbage. Weight it down with a heavy stone and leave for 1 week.

Rinse the cabbage thoroughly under cold running water, then squeeze out as much moisture as possible. Slice into 2.5 cm (1 in) sections or chop more finely if preferred and put into the cleaned pot, this time layering with the spring onion, garlic, chilli and ginger. Fill the pot with the combined dashi and soy sauce. Cover with baking paper, cover with a lid, and refrigerate.

After 4–5 days the kim chi is ready for eating. Serve with hot white rice and a dash of soy sauce.

Note

In cold weather kim chi does not require refrigeration, but when the weather is warm, store in the refrigerator for up to 3 weeks.

Oyi Namul
Cucumber salad

Serves: 6

2 telegraph (long) cucumbers, peeled and
thinly sliced

3 teaspoons coarse salt

2 tablespoons rice vinegar or mild white
vinegar

1 teaspoon sugar

¼ teaspoon cayenne pepper

1 garlic clove, finely chopped

1 spring onion (scallion), finely chopped

3 teaspoons toasted, crushed sesame seeds

Put the cucumber into a bowl, sprinkle with the salt and add
250 ml (8½ fl oz/1 cup) water. Leave to soak for 15 minutes,
then drain well.

In a bowl, combine all the other ingredients, pour over the
cucumbers, mix well and serve chilled.

Kong Namul
Bean sprout salad

Serves: 6

390 g (14 oz/4⅓ cups) fresh mung or soy bean sprouts, trimmed

1 tablespoon sesame oil

1 tablespoon salad oil

1 tablespoon toasted, crushed sesame seeds

60 ml (2 fl oz/¼ cup) light soy sauce

1 garlic clove, crushed

2 spring onions (scallions), thinly sliced

1 teaspoon honey or sugar

1 pinch of chilli powder or cayenne pepper

Blanch the bean sprouts in a saucepan of lightly salted boiling water for 1 minute if using mung beans, or slightly longer for soy beans. The sprouts should be just tender. Drain well, refresh in cold water and drain again.

In a bowl, combine all the other ingredients. Add the bean sprouts and toss to coat in the dressing. Chill before serving.

Glossary
and Index

❖

Aburage (deep-fried tofu sheets)

Japanese-style deep-fried tofu. Unlike the Chinese type (*dow foo pok*), which comes in cubes, aburage is prepared in thin square or rectangular sheets, which can be split to form a pocket and then stuffed with sushi rice. Sold refrigerated, it can be frozen and stored for months. *See also tofu.*

Bamboo Shoots

Sold in tins and jars, either water-packed, pickled or braised. Unless otherwise stated, the recipes in this book use the water-packed variety. If using the tinned variety, store left-over bamboo shoots in a bowl of fresh water in the refrigerator, changing the water daily for up to 10 days. Winter bamboo shoots are much smaller and more tender, and are called for in certain recipes. However, if they are not available, use the larger variety. Also known as: *wah-bho-khmyit* (Burma), *tumpeang* (Cambodia), *suehn* (China), *rebung* (Indonesia), *takenoko* (Japan), *rebong* (Malaysia), *labong* (Philippines), *normai* (Thailand), *mang* (Vietnam).

Bean sprouts

Green mung beans are traditionally used for bean sprouts. They are sold fresh in most large supermarkets, Asian grocery stores and health food stores. Chinese stores sell longer shoots than those available from supermarkets, which are usually just starting to sprout. Substitute thinly sliced celery for a similar texture but different flavour. Very fresh bean sprouts can be stored in the refrigerator for up to 4 days in a plastic bag; alternatively, cover with water and change the water daily. Before using, rinse the sprouts, drain well and trim off the brown tails. Also known as: *pepinauk* (Burma), *nga choi* (China), *taoge* (Indonesia), *moyashi* (Japan), *suk ju* (Korea), *taugeh* (Malaysia and Singapore), *tau ngork* (Thailand), *gia* (Vietnam).

Bonito

A fish, often called Pacific bonito, whose dried flesh is used as a base for many Japanese broths and stocks. It is sold in blocks or as very thin shavings. It is also sold as granules for making dashi. Also known as: *nga-kyi-kan* (Burma), *balaki, tongkol* (Indonesia), *katuso* (Japan), *kayau* (Malaysia), *rayado* (Philippines), *balaya* (Sri Lanka), *pla o* (Thailand), *ca bo* (Vietnam). *See also bonito flakes and dashi.*

Bonito flakes (katsuobushi)

Dried bonito is the favourite flavouring ingredient in Japanese cooking. It can be bought already flaked; this is by far the most convenient, for dried bonito is extremely hard and needs a special tool for shaving it.

Cellophane (bean thread) noodles

These are fine, translucent noodles made from the starch of green mung beans. The noodles may be soaked in hot water before use, or may require boiling according to the texture required. They can also be deep-fried straight from the packet, generally when used as a garnish or to provide a background for other foods. Also known as: *kyazan* (Burma), *mee sooer* (Cambodia), *bi fun, ning fun, sai fun, fun see* (China), *sotanghoon* (Indonesia), *harusame* (Japan), *sohoon, tunghoon* (Malaysia), *sotanghon* (Philippines), *woon sen* (Thailand), *búng u, mien* (Vietnam).

Chillies, green and red

Botanical name: *Capsicum* spp.
Chillies mature from green to red, becoming hotter as they mature. Both varieties are used fresh for flavouring, either whole or finely chopped, sliced as a garnish or ground into sambals. The seeds, which are the hottest parts, are usually (though not always) removed. Larger varieties tend to be milder than the small varieties. See page 7 for handling. Dried red chillies are found in packets in Asian grocery stores – the medium- to large-sized chillies are best for most recipes in this book.

Chilli powder

Asian chilli powder is made from ground chillies. It is much hotter than the Mexican-style chilli powder, which is mostly ground cumin. You may be able to find ground Kashmiri chillies, which are a brighter red colour and not as hot as other ground chillies.

Chinese bean sauce

Most bean sauces are too thick to pour as they are a paste consistency. There are many types of bean sauce. In Chinese cooking, ground bean sauce (*mor sze jeung*) has a smooth texture and can be used as a substitute for Korean bean sauce in cooking. Another type, *min sze jeung*, is a thick paste of mashed fermented soy beans and is similar to Malaysian taucheo. Whenever bean sauce is an ingredient in recipes from Malaysia, Singapore and China, use *min sze jeung* if possible. Substitute mashed salted black beans, sold in tins. Other variations include Chinese chilli bean sauce, sweet bean sauce and hot bean sauce.

Coriander (cilantro)

Botanical name: *Coriandrum sativum*
All parts of the coriander (cilantro) plant are used in Asian cooking. The dried seed is the main ingredient in curry powder, and although not hot it has a fragrance that makes it an essential part of a curry blend. The fresh coriander herb is also known as cilantro or Chinese parsley in other parts of the world. It is indispensable in Burma, Thailand, Vietnam, Cambodia, India and China where it is also called 'fragrant green'. Also known as: *nannamzee* (seed), *nannambin* (leaves) (Burma), *chee van soy* (Cambodia), *yuen sai* (China), *dhania* (seed), *dhania pattar, dhania sabz* (leaves) (India), *phak hom pom* (Laos), *ketumbar* (seeds), *daun ketumbar* (leaves) (Malaysia), *kinchay* (Philippines), *kottamalli* (seed), *kottamalli kolle* (leaves) (Sri Lanka), *pak chee* (Thailand), *ngò, rau mùi* (Vietnam).

Daikon (white radish)

Botanical name: *Raphanus sativus*

Daikon is a very large white radish most popularly known by its Japanese name and it is about 30–38 cm (12–15¼ in) long with a mild flavour. It is sold in Asian grocery stores and some large greengrocers and supermarkets. Substitute white turnip if not available. Also known as: *loh hahk* (China), *muuli* (India), *lobak* (Indonesia and Malaysia), *mu* (*moo*) (Korea), *labanos* (Philippines), *rabu* (Sri Lanka), *phakkat-hua* (Thailand), *cù cải trng* (Vietnam).

Dashi

A clear soup made from dried bonito flakes and seaweed. Instant dashi, sold in Japanese grocery stores, is made from bonito flakes (katsuobushi) and kombu (dried kelp). It is essential for Japanese cooking – in addition to being served as a soup it is used as a cooking stock or as part of a dipping sauce.

Fish cakes, Japanese-style (kamaboko)

Both Chinese-style fish cakes and Japanese-style fish cakes are sold ready to use in most Asian grocery stores. They can be kept for a few days if refrigerated, and need no further cooking apart from heating through.

Ginger

Botanical name: *Zingiber officinale*

A rhizome with a robust flavour and a warming quality, it is essential in most Asian dishes. Fresh ginger root should be used; powdered ginger cannot be substituted for fresh ginger, for the flavour is quite different. To prepare for use, scrape off the skin with a sharp knife and either grate or chop finely (according to recipe requirements) before measuring. To preserve fresh ginger for long periods of time, place in a freezer bag and store in the freezer – it is a simple matter to peel and grate in the frozen state. *See also pickled ginger (beni shoga).* Also known as: *gin* (Burma), *khnyahee* (Cambodia), *jeung* (China), *adrak* (India), *jahe* (Indonesia), *shoga* (Japan), *halia* (Malaysia), *luya* (Philippines), *inguru* (Sri Lanka), *khing* (Thailand), *gung* (Vietnam).

Ginkgo nuts

Botanical name: *Ginkgo biloba*

The kernel of the fruit of the maidenhair tree, which grows in China and Japan. It has an individual and slightly bitter flavour, and is eaten roasted as a nut or used to give its flavour to foods. Usually sold tinned or shrink-sealed, it may also be labelled 'white nut'. Before eating, fresh nuts need to have their outer layer removed and then should be boiled for about 30 minutes or they can be toxic. The nut, or seed of the fruit in its shell, looks a little like a large, closed pistachio nut. Also known as: *bahk gwoah* (China), *ginnan* (Japan).

Gomashio (sesame salt)

A seasoning of black sesame seeds, coarse salt and Monosodium Glutamate (MSG) used in Japanese cooking.

Harusame noodles

Fine Japanese noodles, made from bean starch, that are translucent when soaked and boiled. When deep-fried from the dried state they become crisp, white and opaque, and puff up. They are the equivalent of China's *fen szu* or cellophane (bean thread) noodles. See notes on noodles (pages 9–10).

Hijiki

Botanical name: *Cystophyllum fusiforme*

A type of seaweed used as a vegetable by the Japanese. In its dried state it looks like coarse black wire. It must be soaked before cooking.

Kombu (dried kelp)

Botanical name: *Laminaria japonica*

Japanese kelp seaweed, available dried in broad, greyish black ribbons. It is used to flavour dashi and rice used for sushi. It will keep indefinitely, and is also pickled to be used as a relish.

Lotus root

Botanical name: *Nelumbo nucifera*

The edible rhizome of the graceful, ancient flowering water plant. Sometimes available fresh; peel, cut into slices and use as directed. Dried lotus root must be soaked for at least 20 minutes in hot water with a little lemon juice added to preserve whiteness. Peeled and sliced frozen lotus root is widely available. Tinned lotus root can be stored in the refrigerator for a few days after being opened. The seeds of the spent flower, peeled and eaten raw as a snack in Asia, are mild-tasting with a subtle crunch. The dried seeds, sometimes known as 'lotus nuts', must be boiled until soft. They are crystallised with sugar as part of Chinese New Year sweet offerings, cooked into a sweet soup, and made into sweetened lotus nut paste, which is mostly sold in tins and used as a filling for Chinese moon cakes. Also known as: *lien ngow, ngau* (China), *kamal-kakri* (India), *teratai* (Indonesia), *renkon* (Japan), *seroja* (Malaysia), *baino* (Philippines), *nelun-ala* (Sri Lanka), *bua-luang* (Thailand).

Mirin

Japanese rice wine that is sweeter than sake and used only for cooking. Dry sherry can be used as a substitute.

Miso

A paste made from cooked, fermented soy beans. There are various types: white, red, brownish and beige – with white and red being the main ones. There are also varying degrees of saltiness, so make sure you allow for it. Japanese thick soups are mostly based on miso stirred into dashi, the usual proportion being 1 tablespoon to 250 ml (8½ fl oz/1 cup) of stock. There is also a yellow bean paste used in Singapore and Indonesia called *taucheo*.

Mushrooms, shiitake (dried)

Botanical name: *Lentinus edodes*
Also known as 'fragrant mushrooms', the flavour of these mushrooms is quite individual. They are expensive but give an incomparable flavour. Soak for 20–30 minutes before using. The stems are usually discarded and only the caps used. There is no substitute. Also known as: *hmo chauk* (Burma), *doong gwoo, leong goo* (China), *cindauwan* (Malaysia), *kabuteng shiitakena pinatuyo* (Philippines), *hed hom* (Thailand), *khô nm shiitake, nm ro'm khô* (Vietnam).

Nori

Botanical name: *Pophyra tenera, P. umbilicalis*
Dried laver, a type of edible seaweed, which is one of the most popular flavourings, garnishes and decorations in Japanese cooking. It is sold in paper-thin sheets, is shiny purple-black in colour, and must be warmed and crisped before use.

Oyster sauce

Adds delicate flavour to all kinds of dishes. Made from oysters cooked in soy sauce and brine, this thick brown sauce can be kept indefinitely in the refrigerator. Also known as: *ho yu* (China).

Panko (Japanese breadcrumbs)

Panko, or Japanese breadcrumbs, are not like Western-style breadcrumbs at all and, if a recipe requires them, don't try to substitute any other. They are large, light and give a crispness, which cannot be duplicated. They are sold in packets in Japanese stores.

Peanut oil

A traditional cooking medium in Chinese and Southeast Asian countries. Asian unrefined peanut oil is highly flavoured and more expensive than the refined peanut oil found in Western supermarkets. It has a high smoking point and adds a distinctive flavour to stir-fries. Refined peanut oil is ideal for deep-frying. Take all the usual precautions where peanuts are concerned and avoid it if cooking for anyone with nut sensitivities. Use olive oil flavoured with a little sesame oil as an alternative.

Pepper, black

Botanical name: *Piper nigrum*
Pepper, the berry of a tropical vine native to India, is green when immature, and red or yellow when ripe. Black pepper is obtained by boiling and then sun-drying the green, unripe drupes. It is only used in some curries, but is an important ingredient in

garam masala. Vietnam is the main producer of pepper. Also known as: *nga-youk-kaun* (Burma), *hu-chiao* (China), *kali mirich* (India), *merica hitam* (Indonesia), *kosho* (Japan), *phik noi* (Laos), *lada hitam* (Malaysia), *paminta* (Philippines), *gammiris* (Sri Lanka), *prik thai* (Thailand).

Perilla

Botanical name: *Lamiaceae, Perilla frustescens* and *crispa*
Perilla, known as shiso in Japan, is a relative of mint and basil with a stronger, spicier flavour. There are green and red varieties. Often served with raw fish as it is believed to counteract food poisoning. Also known as: *la tia to* (Vietnam).

Pickled ginger (beni shoga)

Pickled ginger, coloured bright red, and sold in plastic packets or in bottles. Used as a garnish or for flavour.

Rice vermicelli (rice-stick) noodles

These are very fine rice flour noodles sold in Chinese grocery stores. Soaking in hot water for 10 minutes prepares them sufficiently for most recipes, but in some cases they may need boiling for 1–2 minutes. When deep-fried they swell up and turn white. For a crisp result, fry them straight from the packet without soaking. Also known as: *mee sooer* (Cambodia), *mei fun* (China), *beehoon, meehoon* (Malaysia), *sen mee* (Thailand), *bún, lúa min* (Vietnam).

Rice vinegar

Made from fermented rice, this vinegar is popular in China, Japan and Korea. Although rice vinegar was originally made from rice cooked with water then treated with yeast to ferment the sugar in the grain, these days it is usually made from rice wine lees and alcohol. Adding sugar also speeds up the process. Dilute white wine vinegar or cider vinegar if you can't get the real thing.

Sake

Pronounced sahk-ay, Japan's famous rice wine is usually served warm – about 44°C (111°F) – easily achieved by immersing the wine's container in very hot water for a short time. It is also used as an ingredient in sauces and marinades, when brandy or dry sherry can be substituted.

Sansho (Japanese pepper)

Botanical name: *Zanthoxylum* spp.
The pod of the prickly ash, dried and ground, gives a slightly hot flavour to certain Japanese foods, especially rich foods like eel. It is used to counter fatty tastes. Sansho is only available ground.

Sesame oil

The sesame oil used in Chinese, Japanese and Korean cooking is extracted from toasted sesame seeds and has a different flavour from the lighter-coloured sesame oil sold in health food stores. For the recipes in this book, buy sesame oil from Asian grocery stores. Use the oil in small quantities for flavouring, not as a cooking medium. Also known as: *hnan zi* (Burma), *ma yau* (China), *gingelly, til ka tel* (India), *goma abura* (Japan), *chan keh room* (Korea), *minyak bijan* (Malaysia), *thala tel* (Sri Lanka), *dau me* (Vietnam).

Sesame seeds

Used mostly in Korean, Chinese and Japanese food, and in sweets in other Southeast Asian countries. Black sesame, another variety known as *hak chih mah* (China) or *kuro goma* (Japan), is mainly used in the Chinese dessert, toffee apples, and as a flavouring (gomashio/sesame salt) mixed with salt in Japanese food. Also known as: *hnan si* (Burma), *til, gingelly* (India), *wijen* (Indonesia), *keh* (Korea), *bijan* (Malaysia), *linga* (Philippines), *thala* (Sri Lanka), *nga dee la* (Thailand), *me* (Vietnam).

Shirataki noodles

These translucent noodles, used in sukiyaki, are also referred to as white waterfall. Made from the starch of the tuberous root *Amorphophallus konjack*, sometimes called 'devil's tongue', they are included in many soups and wet dishes. Also known as *konnyaku* or *konjack*, they are prized for their unique texture and translucent whiteness. They are usually sold in tins or floating in sealed plastic packets, ready to rinse and use in Japanese cooking.

Shiso

See perilla.

Soba noodles

Very fine buckwheat noodles used in Japanese cooking. See notes on noodles (pages 9-10).

Somen noodles

Very fine white wheat flour noodles used in Japanese cooking. As a substitute use very fine vermicelli. See notes on noodles (pages 9-10).

Soy sauce

Indispensable in Asian cooking, this versatile sauce enhances the flavour of every basic ingredient in a dish. Different grades are available. Chinese cooking uses light soy and dark soy. The light soy is used with chicken or seafoods, or in soups where the delicate colour of the dish must be retained. Always use shoyu (Japanese soy sauce) in Japanese cooking. In Indonesia, kecap manis, a thick, dark, sweetened soy, is often used. As a substitute, use dark Chinese soy with black or brown sugar added in the proportions given in recipes. All types of soy sauce keep indefinitely without refrigeration.

Spring onions (scallions)

Botanical name: *Allium cepa* and *fistulum*

Also known as green onions in some parts of the world, this member of the onion family is known as a 'shallot' in some areas of Australia, but is correctly called a spring onion almost everywhere else – although the term 'scallion' is popular in the United States. Spring onions are the thinnings of either *Allium cepa* or *A. fistulum* plantings that do not form a bulb. They are white and slender with green leaves, and are used widely in China and Japan. Also known as: *da cong, tai tsung* (China), *hari piaz* (India), *daun bawang* (Indonesia), *negi* (Japan), *phak boua sot* (Laos), *daun bawang* (Malaysia), *sibuyas na tagsibol* (Philippines), *ton hom* (Thailand), *hanh la* (Vietnam).

Takuan (pickled daikon/white radish)

Pickled daikon (white radish); widely used in Japanese cooking. It is available from Asian grocery stores and those specialising in Japanese ingredients.

Tofu

There is an abundance of varieties of this versatile soy product available. Fresh tofu, or bean curd, is found in the refrigerator section of Asian grocery stores and most large supermarkets. It comes in many forms: silken, soft or firm. Silken tofu is sweeter and more delicate than firm tofu, with a different texture and flavour. Once opened, tofu will keep for 2–3 days in the refrigerator if immersed in cold water that is changed daily. Dried tofu is sold in flat sheets or rounded sticks and needs no refrigeration. It has to be soaked before use – the sticks need longer soaking and cooking. Deep-fried tofu puffs are also available. Red tofu is much more pungent than fresh tofu, and has a flavour like smelly cheese. It is sold in bottles and used in certain sauces. *See also aburage.* Also known as: *dow foo, doufu, doufu-ru* (China), *tahu* (Indonesia), *doufu-kan, abura-age, yuba* (Japan), *taukwa* (Malaysia), *tojo, tokua* (Philippines), *tao hu, forng tao hu* (Thailand), *dau hu* (Vietnam).

Udon noodles

Thick wheat flour noodles used in Japanese cooking. See notes on noodles (see page 14).

Wakame

Botanical name: *Undaria pinnatifida*
A type of seaweed with long, narrow ribbon-like strands. Sold dried, it must be soaked before use in Japanese cooking. It is used in soups and relishes.

Wasabi

Botanical name: *Wasabia japonica*
A pungent green horseradish used by the Japanese. It is available ready to use as a paste sold in tubes or in dried, powdered form in tins. It is reconstituted (like dry mustard) by the addition of a little cold water.

Water chestnuts

Botanical name: *Eliocharis dulcis*
Used mainly for their texture in Asian cooking. Sometimes available fresh, their brownish black skin must be peeled away with a sharp knife, leaving the crisp, slightly sweet white kernel. They are also available in tins, already peeled and in some instances sliced. After opening, store in water in the refrigerator for 7–10 days, changing the water daily. Yam bean (jicama) may be substituted if water chestnut is unavailable. Dried, powdered water chestnut starch is used as an alternative to cornflour (cornstarch) for coating delicate meat such as chicken breast when deep-frying, as it helps lock in the juices. Also known as: *ye thit eir thee* (Burma), *mah tai* (China), *pani phul* (India), *tike* (Indonesia), *kuwai, kurogu-wai* (Japan), *apulid* (Philippines), *haeo-song krathiem, haeo cheen* (Thailand), *go nung* (Vietnam).

Winter bamboo shoots

See bamboo shoots.

Won ton wrappers

Small squares of fresh noodle dough available at most supermarkets and Asian grocery stores. They can be refrigerated for up to 1 week if well wrapped in plastic, or can be wrapped in foil and frozen. Sold by weight, there are approximately 60 wrappers to a 300 g (10½ oz) packet.

Glossary

INDEX

A

aburage 119
agedashi tofu 70
Appetisers 82
Asian food 5

B

baechu 72
bamboo mats 14
bamboo shoots 119
Banquet firepot 106
barbecue 74
Barbecued short ribs of beef 99
basmati rice 8
bean curd *see* tofu
bean paste 72
bean sauces 119
bean sprouts 119
  Bean sprout salad 117
  Soup of soy bean sprouts 88
bean thread noodles 10, 119
beans 73
  Bean pancakes 83
  Bean paste soup 34
  Chinese bean sauce 119
  Green beans with prawns 90
beef 73
  Appetisers 82
  Barbecued short ribs of beef 99
  Beef and spring onions on skewers 60
  Beef stew 97
  Beef stock 84
  Beef tataki with ponzu sauce 30
  Beef teriyaki 61
  Beef and vegetable soup 85
  Braised beef with onions 102
  Deep-fried beef slices 98
  Fiery beef 100
  Grilled marinated beef 61
  Meat and seafood on the griddle 58
  Oxtail soup 84
  Quick-cooked beef and vegetables 57
  Rare seared beef 30
  Simmered steak and vegetables 63

Skewered beef and mushrooms 105
Stir-fried beef with fresh mushrooms 103
Stir-fried cucumbers with beef 108
Stir-fried mixture 109
bindaettoek 83
black pepper 121
bokum bahb 77
bonito 119
  dried/smoked 13
bonito flakes (katsuobushi) 119
Braised beef with onions 102
Braised chicken and mushrooms 95
Braised spinach with pork 110
breadcrumbs, Japanese 121
bulgalbi 99
bulgogi 100
Bulgogi sauce 100

C

cabbage
  baechu 72
  Daikon and cabbage salad 69
  Dumpling soup 86
  Fried and steamed dumplings 29
  Pickled Chinese cabbage 114
California rolls 26
cellophane noodles 10, 119
chap chye 109
chawan mushi 49
chicken
  Braised chicken and mushrooms 95
  Chicken omelette 52
  Chicken stew 96
  Chicken stock 32
  Chicken teriyaki 56
  Chicken and vegetable soup (1) 38
  Chicken and vegetable soup (2) 38
  Fried chicken with sesame 54
  Grilled marinated chicken 56
  Hearty noodle soup 36
  Marinated fried chicken 54
  Parent and child domburi 18
  Rice with chicken and mushrooms 51
  Rice with fried chicken 55
  Steamed egg custard with chicken 49
  Steamed mushrooms with prawn and chicken 111

chickens, jointing 10
Chilled noodles 20
Chilli dipping sauce 29
chilli powder 119
chillies 7, 119
  dried 7
  seeds 7, 119
Chinese bean sauce 119
chirashi-zushi 23
cho kanjang 82
chopsticks 14, 74
cilantro 119–20
confectionery 74
Cooked rice 17
coriander 119–20
Crab and pork fried rice 77
cucumber
  Cucumber salad 116
  Stir-fried cucumbers with beef 108
  Vinegared cucumber 68
curry powder 119
Custard 49, 65

D

daikon (white radish) 72, 120
  Daikon and cabbage salad 69
  Daikon salad 113
  pickled daikon 123
dak busutjim 95
dak jim 96
dashi 32, 120
dashi, Tofu in 70
Dashi stock 32, 120
dashimaki tamago 35
Deep-fried beef slices 98
Deep-fried seafood 45
Deep-fried seafood and vegetables 46
deep-frying 7
  checking temperature 7
  oils for 7
dhwen-jang 72
dried cellophane noodles 10
dried egg noodles 9
dried rice noodles 9
dried rice vermicelli noodles 9
dumplings
  Dumpling soup 86

Index ❖